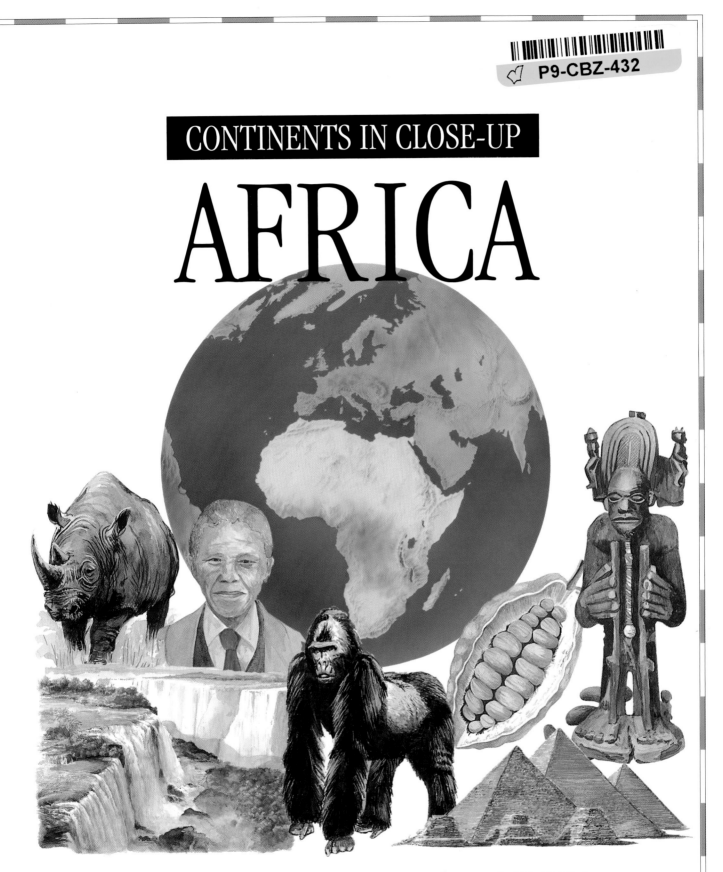

CONTINENTS IN CLOSE-UP

AFRICA

MALCOLM PORTER and KEITH LYE

RAINTREE
STECK-VAUGHN
PUBLISHERS

A Cherrytree Book
Designed and produced by
AS Publishing
Text by Keith Lye
Illustrated by Malcolm Porter and Raymond Turvey

First published 1999
by Cherrytree Press Limited

First published in the United States 2002
by Raintree Steck-Vaughn Publishers

Library of Congress Cataloging-in-Publication Data

Porter, Malcolm.
   Africa / Malcolm Porter and Keith Lye.
      p. cm. - - (Continents in close-up)
   Originally published: Bath [England] : Cherrytree
   Books, 1999, in series: Continents in close-up.
   Includes index.
   ISBN 0-7398-3240-9
   1. Africa - - Juvenile literature. [1. Africa.] I. Lye,
   Keith. II. Title. III. Continents in close-up
   (Austin, Tex.)

   DT3 .P67 2001
   960 - -dc21
                                  2001019557
   ISBN 0-7398-3240-9

Printed in Hong Kong

CONTINENTS IN CLOSE-UP
AFRICA

This illustrated atlas combines maps, pictures, flags, globes, information panels, diagrams, and charts to give an overview of the whole continent and a closer look at each of its countries.

COUNTRY CLOSE-UPS

Each double-page spread has these features:

Introduction The author introduces the most important facts about the country or region.

Globes A globe on which you can see the country's position in the continent and the world.

Flags Every country's flag is shown.

Information panels Every country has an information panel, which gives its area, population, and capital, and where possible its currency, religions, languages, main towns, and government.

Pictures Important features of each country are illustrated and captioned to give a flavor of the country. You can find out about physical features, famous people, ordinary people, animals, plants, places, products, and much more.

Maps Every country is shown on a clear, accurate map. To get the most out of the maps it helps to know the symbols, which are shown in the key on the opposite page.

Land You can see by the coloring on the map where the land is forested, frozen, or desert.

Height Relief hill shading shows where the mountain ranges are. Individual mountains are marked by a triangle.

Direction All of the maps are drawn with north at the top of the page.

Scale All of the maps are drawn to scale so that you can find the distance between places in miles or kilometers.

0	200 miles
0	200 kilometers

KEY TO MAPS

KENYA	Country name
~~	Country border
▪	More than 1 million people*
•	More than 500,000 people
·	Less than 500,000 people
☐	Country capital
ATLAS MTS	Mountain range
▲ Kilimanjaro 19,435 feet (5,895 m)	Mountain with its height

Many large cities, such as Johannesburg, have metropolitan populations that are greater than the city figures. Such cities have larger dot sizes to emphasize their importance.

Nile	River
~+~+~	Canal
⬬	Lake
—+—	Dam
⬭	Island

	Forest
	Crops
	Dry grassland
	Desert
	Tundra
	Polar

CONTINENT CLOSE-UPS

People and Beliefs Map of population densities; chart of percentage of population by country; chart of areas of countries; map of religions; chart of main religious groups.

Climate and Vegetation Map of vegetation from forest to desert; maps of winter and summer temperatures; map of annual rainfall.

Ecology and Environment Map and panel on environmental damage to land and sea; map of natural hazards and diseases; panel on endangered species.

Economy Map of agricultural and industrial products; pie-chart of gross national product for individual countries; panel on per capita gross national products; map and panel on sources of energy.

Politics and History Map showing pre-colonial events, slave trade routes and areas of recent conflicts; panel of great events; timeline of important dates; map of European colonies in 1913; flag of the Organization of African Unity.

Index All the names on the maps and in the picture captions can be found in the index at the end of the book.

CONTENTS

Chimpanzee
See page 17

AFRICA

Africa, the second-largest continent, is changing quickly. As recently as 50 years ago, European nations ruled most of Africa. As these former colonies became independent, the new governments emerged and new names appeared on the map of Africa.

Many countries adopted one-party governments. Others suffered civil war and came under military dictators. Above all, Africa faced a struggle against poverty; many of its countries are still among the world's poorest. Farming is the main activity, but many farmers produce little more than they need to support their families. Mining is important, but most of Africa lacks industries.

Democracy has been hard-won in many African countries. Nelson Mandela became president of South Africa in 1994. The 28 years he spent in prison for his opposition to apartheid (separation of the races) in South Africa made him an international symbol of liberty.

People South of the Sahara the continent is populated mostley by black Africans, who speak more than 1,000 local languages. By contrast, in North Africa, the Arab and Berber people mostly speak Arabic. In much of Africa, poverty and disease—especially AIDS—is widespread, and the average and life expectancy is less than 50 years.

Spectacular sights attract a large number of tourists to Africa. Victoria Falls, on the border between Zambia and Zimbabwe, is one of Africa's many scenic attractions. Local people call it Mosi-oa-tunya, or ''the smoke that thunders.''

Mediterranean Sea

NORTH ATLANTIC OCEAN

MOROCCO

TUNISIA

ALGERIA

Western Sahara

MAURITANIA

MALI

NIGER

CAPE VERDE

SENEGAL

GAMBIA

BURKINA FASO

GUINEA-BISSAU

GUINEA

BENIN

NIGERIA

IVORY COAST

TOGO

SIERRA LEONE

GHANA

LIBERIA

CAMEROON

EQUATORIAL GUINEA

SAO TOME & PRINCIPE

GABON

REPUBLIC OF CONGO

CABINDA (Angola)

NAMIBIA

SOUTH ATLANTIC OCEAN

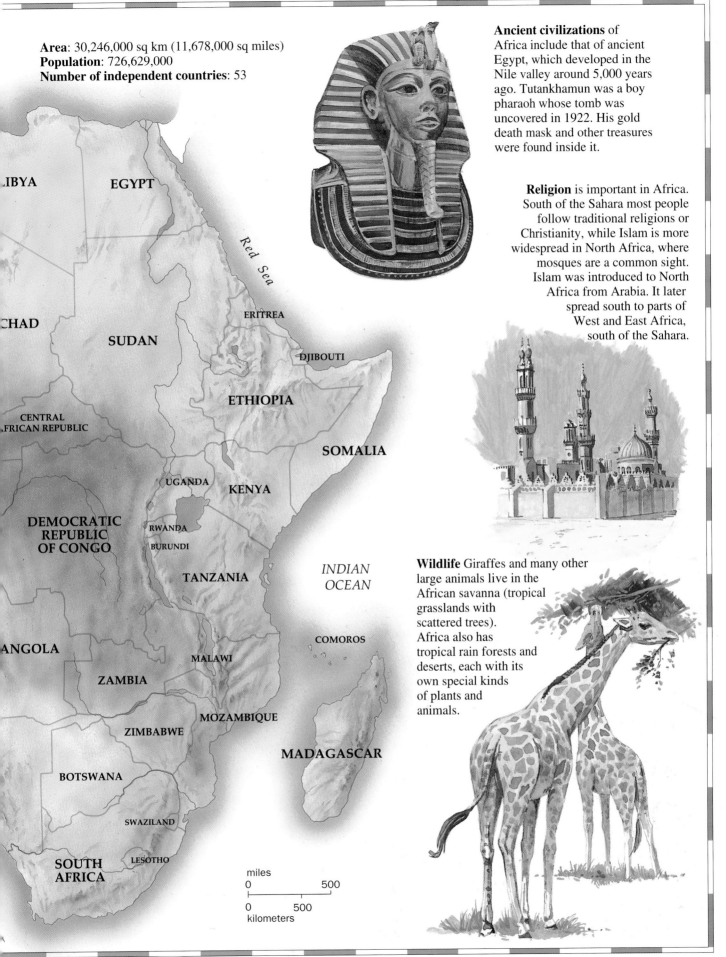

Area: 30,246,000 sq km (11,678,000 sq miles)
Population: 726,629,000
Number of independent countries: 53

Ancient civilizations of Africa include that of ancient Egypt, which developed in the Nile valley around 5,000 years ago. Tutankhamun was a boy pharaoh whose tomb was uncovered in 1922. His gold death mask and other treasures were found inside it.

Religion is important in Africa. South of the Sahara most people follow traditional religions or Christianity, while Islam is more widespread in North Africa, where mosques are a common sight. Islam was introduced to North Africa from Arabia. It later spread south to parts of West and East Africa, south of the Sahara.

Wildlife Giraffes and many other large animals live in the African savanna (tropical grasslands with scattered trees). Africa also has tropical rain forests and deserts, each with its own special kinds of plants and animals.

LIBYA
EGYPT
Red Sea
ERITREA
CHAD
SUDAN
DJIBOUTI
ETHIOPIA
CENTRAL AFRICAN REPUBLIC
SOMALIA
UGANDA
KENYA
DEMOCRATIC REPUBLIC OF CONGO
RWANDA
BURUNDI
INDIAN OCEAN
TANZANIA
ANGOLA
COMOROS
MALAWI
ZAMBIA
MOZAMBIQUE
ZIMBABWE
MADAGASCAR
BOTSWANA
SWAZILAND
SOUTH AFRICA
LESOTHO

miles
0   500

0   500
kilometers

5

NORTHWESTERN AFRICA

Northwestern Africa consists of three countries –Algeria, Morocco, and Tunisia–and one territory, called Western Sahara. Western Sahara was once ruled by Spain and called Spanish Sahara. It is now occupied by Morocco, but many of its people have fought to make their country independent. The main geographic regions of northwestern Africa are the fertile northern coasts, the high Atlas Mountains, which run through Morocco, Algeria, and Tunisia, and the huge Sahara desert.

Atlas Mountains These high ranges extend about 1,500 miles (2,400 km) across Morocco, Algeria, and northern Tunisia. The highest peak is Jebel Toubkal, in Morocco's High Atlas range.

ALGERIA

Area: 2,381,741 sq km (919,595 sq miles)
Population: 28,734,000
Capital and largest city: Algiers (pop 1,772,000)
Other large cities: Oran (664,000)
Constantine (449,000)
Official language: Arabic
Religion: Islam
Government: Republic
Currency: Algerian dinar

MOROCCO

Area: 446,550 sq km (172,414 sq miles)
Population: 27,020,000
Capital: Rabat (pop 3,200,000)
Other large cities: Casablanca
Marrakesh (602,000)
Official language: Arabic
Religion: Islam
Government: Monarchy
Currency: Moroccan dirham

TUNISIA

Area: 163,610 sq km (63,170 sq miles)
Population: 9,132,000
Capital and largest city: Tunis (pop 674,000)
Other large cities: Sfax (231,000)
Official language: Arabic
Religion: Islam
Government: Republic
Currency: Tunisian dinar

WESTERN SAHARA

Area: 266,000 sq km (102,703 sq miles)
Population: 287,000
Government: Status disputed, but occupied by Morocco

Ceuta
Tangier
Kenitra
Rabat   Fez
Casablanca   Meknès

MOROCCO

ATLANTIC OCEAN

Marrakesh   High Atlas   GRAND
Toubkal
13,665 feet
(4,165 m)
Agadir

CANARY ISLANDS
(Spain)

•Laâyoune

Western Sahara

Ad Dakhla•

Leather goods, such as purses, handbags, shoes and slippers, are made in Morocco. Other major crafts in northwestern Africa include the making of rugs, pottery, and metal goods.

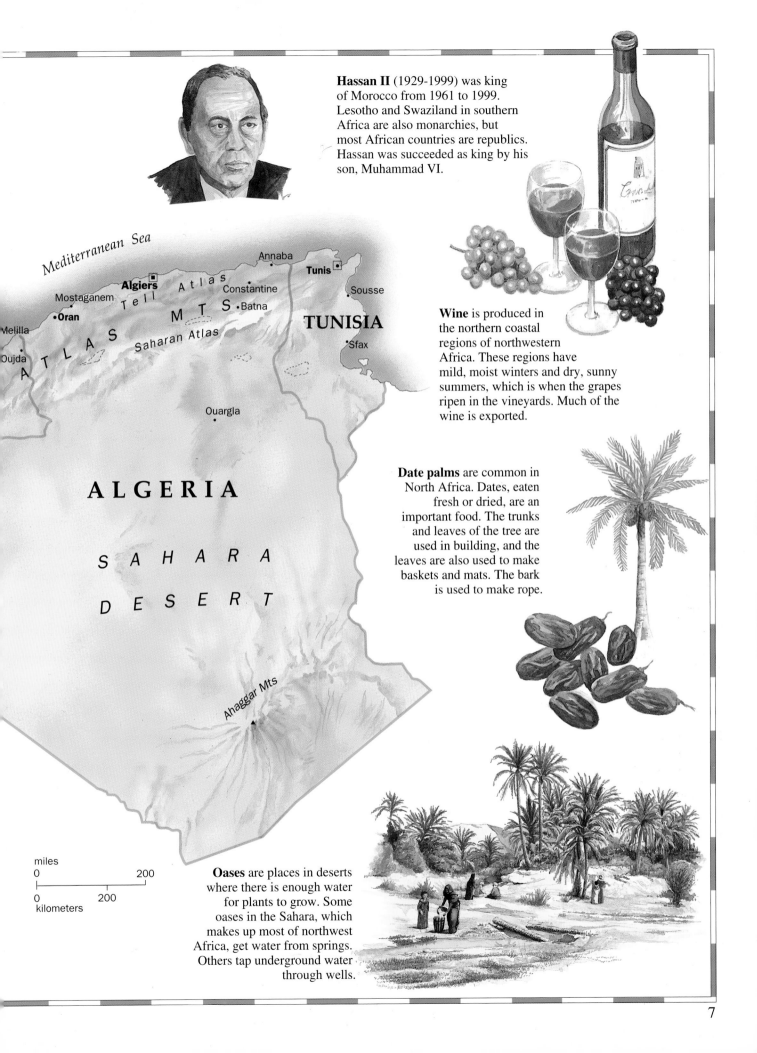

Hassan II (1929-1999) was king of Morocco from 1961 to 1999. Lesotho and Swaziland in southern Africa are also monarchies, but most African countries are republics. Hassan was succeeded as king by his son, Muhammad VI.

Mediterranean Sea

Annaba

Tunis

Sousse

Algiers
Mostaganem
Tell *Atlas*
Constantine

Oran
Melilla
ATLAS
MTS
Batna

TUNISIA

Oujda
Saharan Atlas

Sfax

Ouargla

ALGERIA

S A H A R A

D E S E R T

Ahaggar Mts

Wine is produced in the northern coastal regions of northwestern Africa. These regions have mild, moist winters and dry, sunny summers, which is when the grapes ripen in the vineyards. Much of the wine is exported.

Date palms are common in North Africa. Dates, eaten fresh or dried, are an important food. The trunks and leaves of the tree are used in building, and the leaves are also used to make baskets and mats. The bark is used to make rope.

miles
0 _____ 200
0 _____ 200
kilometers

Oases are places in deserts where there is enough water for plants to grow. Some oases in the Sahara, which makes up most of northwest Africa, get water from springs. Others tap underground water through wells.

7

NORTHEASTERN AFRICA

The Nile valley was the center Ancient Egypt, one of the world's earliest civilizations. Like its oil-rich neighbor Libya, it later became part of the Roman Empire. Other ancient kingdoms developed in Sudan, Africa's largest country. Egypt has some industry, but Sudan is still primarily agricultural. The main religion of the region is Islam. In southern Sudan, where black Africans follow traditional religions or Christianity, many people have fought against rule by the Muslim north.

 **EGYPT**

Area: 1,001,449 sq km (386,662 sq miles)
Population: 59,272,000
Capital and largest cities:
Cairo (pop 9,656,000)
Other large cities: Alexandria (3,380,000)
El Giza (2,144,000)
Official language: Arabic
Religions: Islam 90%, Christianity 10%
Government: Republic
Currency: Egyptian pound

 LIBYA

Area: 1,759,540 sq km (679,362 sq miles)
Population: 5,167,000
Capital: Tripoli (pop 960,000)
Other large cities: Benghazi (472,000)
Official language: Arabic
Religion: Islam
Government: Republic
Currency: Libyan dinar

 **SUDAN**

Area: 2,505,813 sq km (967,500 sq miles)
Population: 27,272,000
Capital: Khartoum (pop 476,000)
Other large cities: Omdurman (526,000)
Khartoum North (341,000)
Official language: Arabic
Religions: Islam 72%, traditional religions 17%, Christianity 11%
Government: Republic
Currency: Sudanese dinar

Tripoli

Misurata

Benghazi

LIBYA

S A H A R A D E S E R T

Oilfields are found in the Sahara in central Libya. Pipelines carry the oil to the coast. Oil accounts for more than 90 per cent of Libya's exports. Egypt produces only enough oil for its own needs.

Cotton is the chief cash crop in Egypt and Sudan. Both produce textiles, including clothes. Egypt also manufactures food products and motor vehicles. It is Africa's second most important industrial country after South Africa.

Colonel Muammar Gaddafi and fellow military officers overthrew the king in Libya in 1969 and took control of the government. Gaddafi used money from oil exports to raise living standards in Libya. He has also given money to some overseas terrorist groups.

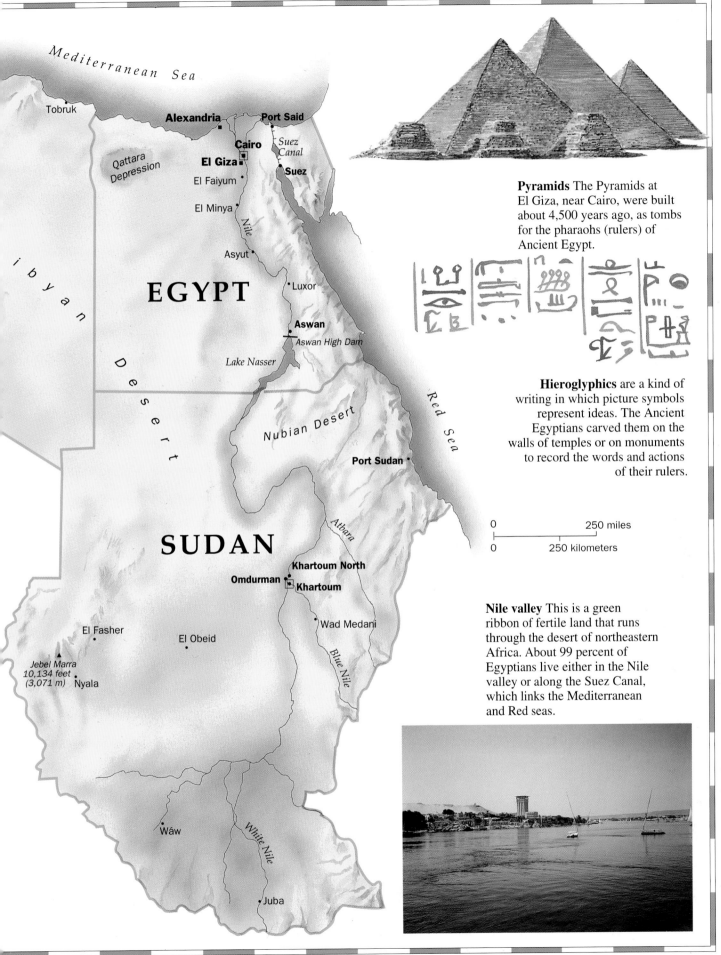

Mediterranean Sea

Tobruk

Alexandria
Port Said

Cairo
Suez Canal

El Giza
Suez

Qattara Depression

El Faiyum

El Minya

Nile

Asyut

EGYPT

Luxor

Libyan Desert

Aswan
Aswan High Dam

Lake Nasser

Nubian Desert

Red Sea

Port Sudan

SUDAN

Atbara

Khartoum North
Omdurman
Khartoum

Wad Medani

El Fasher

El Obeid

Blue Nile

Jebel Marra
10,134 feet
(3,071 m)
Nyala

Wâw

White Nile

Juba

Pyramids The Pyramids at El Giza, near Cairo, were built about 4,500 years ago, as tombs for the pharaohs (rulers) of Ancient Egypt.

Hieroglyphics are a kind of writing in which picture symbols represent ideas. The Ancient Egyptians carved them on the walls of temples or on monuments to record the words and actions of their rulers.

0   250 miles
0   250 kilometers

Nile valley This is a green ribbon of fertile land that runs through the desert of northeastern Africa. About 99 percent of Egyptians live either in the Nile valley or along the Suez Canal, which links the Mediterranean and Red seas.

HORN OF AFRICA

Four countries–Eritrea, Ethiopia, Djibouti, and Somalia–make up the Horn of Africa, so called because on a map it resembles a rhinoceros horn. Ethiopia is a mountainous country, with rain forests in the southwest. But northeastern and southeastern Ethiopia, as well as Eritrea, Djibouti, and Somalia are mostly desert. All the countries are poor. They have suffered in recent years from droughts and civil wars.

ERITREA

Area: 93,680 sq km (36,170 sq miles)
Population: 3,698,000
Capital and largest city: Asmara (pop 400,000)
Official language: None
Religions: Islam 50%, Christianity 50%
Government: Republic
Currency: Nakfa

ETHIOPIA

Area: 1,128,220 sq km (435,608 sq miles)
Population: 58,234,000
Capital and largest city: Addis Ababa (pop 2,113,000)
Official language: None (Amharic is used in government)
Religions: Christianity 57%, Islam 31%, local religions 11%, other 1%
Government: Republic
Currency: Birr

DJIBOUTI

Area: 22,000 sq km (8,494 sq miles)
Population: 619,000
Capital and largest city: Djibouti (pop 383,000)
Official languages: Arabic, French
Religions: Islam 97%, other 3%
Government: Republic
Currency: Djibouti franc

SOMALIA

Area: 637,657 sq km (246,201 sq miles)
Population: 9,805,000
Capital and largest city: Mogadishu (pop 1,000,000)
Official language: Somali
Religion: Islam
Government: Republic
Currency: Somali shilling

Haile Selassie I (1892-1975) was emperor of Ethiopia from 1930 until the monarchy was abolished in 1974. The military group that took over was overthrown in 1991 after a long civil war. Eritrea broke away from Ethiopia to become a separate country in 1993.

Christianity was introduced to Ethiopia in the 4th century. One of its best known churches, at Lalibela in northern Ethiopia, was carved out of solid rock in the 12th and 13th centuries.

Red Sea

Keren
Massawa
Asmara▣

ERITREA

• Aksum
• Mekele
▲ *Ras Dashan* 15,246 feet (4,620 m)
Gonder
Lalibela
Lake Tana
Dese •

ETHIOPIA

Blue Nile

Addis Ababa ▣

Dembi Dolo
Nazret •

Gore
• Jima

Omo
Lake Abaya

• Maji
Lake Chamo

RIFT VALLEY

Lake Stefanie

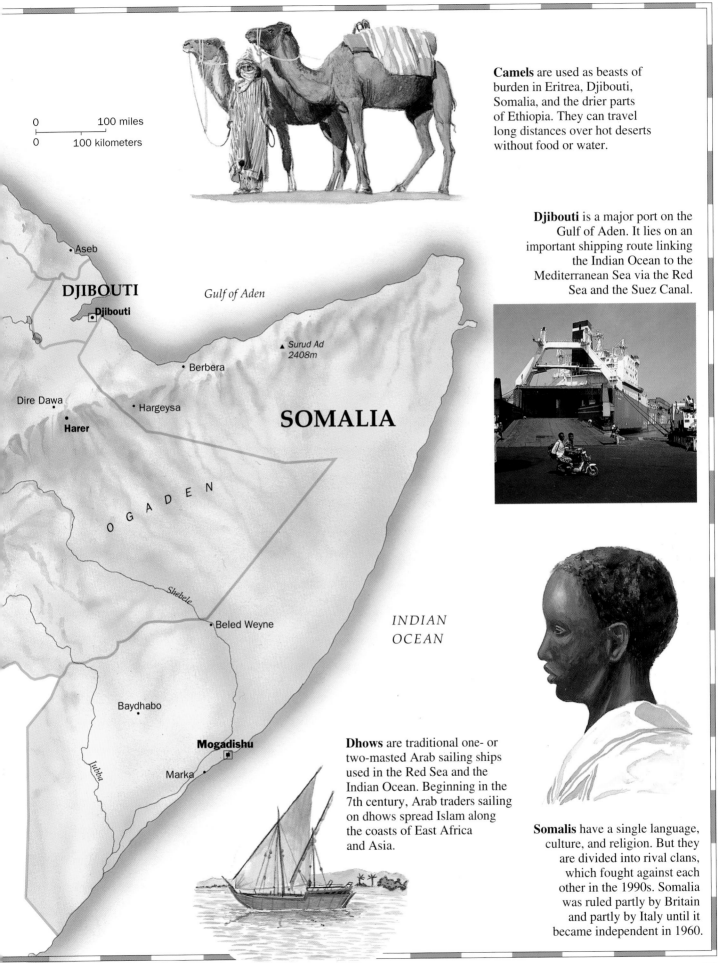

Camels are used as beasts of burden in Eritrea, Djibouti, Somalia, and the drier parts of Ethiopia. They can travel long distances over hot deserts without food or water.

Djibouti is a major port on the Gulf of Aden. It lies on an important shipping route linking the Indian Ocean to the Mediterranean Sea via the Red Sea and the Suez Canal.

0 | 100 miles
0 | 100 kilometers

• Aseb

DJIBOUTI

Gulf of Aden

▪ Djibouti

▲ Surud Ad
2408m

• Berbera

Dire Dawa •

Harer

• Hargeysa

SOMALIA

O G A D E N

Shebele

• Beled Weyne

*INDIAN
OCEAN*

Baydhabo
•

Jubba

Mogadishu
▪

Marka •

Dhows are traditional one- or two-masted Arab sailing ships used in the Red Sea and the Indian Ocean. Beginning in the 7th century, Arab traders sailing on dhows spread Islam along the coasts of East Africa and Asia.

Somalis have a single language, culture, and religion. But they are divided into rival clans, which fought against each other in the 1990s. Somalia was ruled partly by Britain and partly by Italy until it became independent in 1960.

WEST AFRICA 1

West Africa contains 15 countries (5 of which are shown here). Desert covers much of Mauritania and Mali, but southern Mauritania and Mali, together with parts of Senegal and Burkina Faso, lie in a dry grassland region called the Sahel. To the south, the Sahel merges into savanna (tropical grassland with scattered trees). Forests grow along rivers. France once ruled Burkina Faso, Senegal, Mauritania and Mali. Gambia was ruled by Britain until 1965.

MAURITANIA

Area: 1,030,700 sq km (397,956 sq miles)
Population: 2,332,000
Capital and largest city: Nouakchott (pop 600,000)
Official language: Arabic
Religion: Islam
Government: Islamic republic
Currency: Ouguiya

MALI

Area: 1,240,000 sq km (478,767 sq miles)
Population: 9,999,000
Capital and largest city: Bamako (pop 746,000)
Official language: French
Religions: Islam 90%, traditional religions 9%, Christianity 1%
Government: Republic
Currency: CFA franc*

SENEGAL

Area: 196,192 sq km (75,750 sq miles)
Population: 8,534,000
Capital and largest city: Dakar (pop 1,729,000)
Official language: French
Religions: Islam 92%, traditional religions 6%, Christianity 2%
Government: Republic
Currency: CFA franc

GAMBIA

Area: 11,295 sq km (4,361 sq miles)
Population: 1,147,000
Capital and largest city: Banjul (pop 171,000)
Official language: English
Religions: Islam 96%, Christianity 4%
Government: Republic
Currency: Dalasi

Dakar is the capital of Senegal. It is a major port with a fine harbor and is one of Africa's leading industrial cities. The French founded Dakar in 1857 on the site of a fishing village.

Groundnuts are among Gambia's and Senegal's leading exports. In the five countries on this page, more than 80 percent of the people earn their living by farming.

BURKINA FASO

Area: 274,200 sq km (105,869 sq miles)
Population: 10,669,000
Capital and largest city: Ouagadougou (pop 690,000)
Official language: French
Religions: traditional religions (45%), Islam (43%), Christianity 12%
Government: Republic
Currency: CFA franc

* CFA stands for Colonies Françaises d'Afrique

Gambia is a popular holiday spot for tourists from northern Europe. It has good beaches and interesting places to visit on cruises up the Gambia River.

Map labels:
S A
Nouâdhibou
Atâr
MAURITANIA
ATLANTIC OCEAN
Nouakchott
St Louis
SENEGAL
Sénégal
Dakar
Thiès
Kaolack
Banjul
GAMBIA
Gambia
Ziguinchor

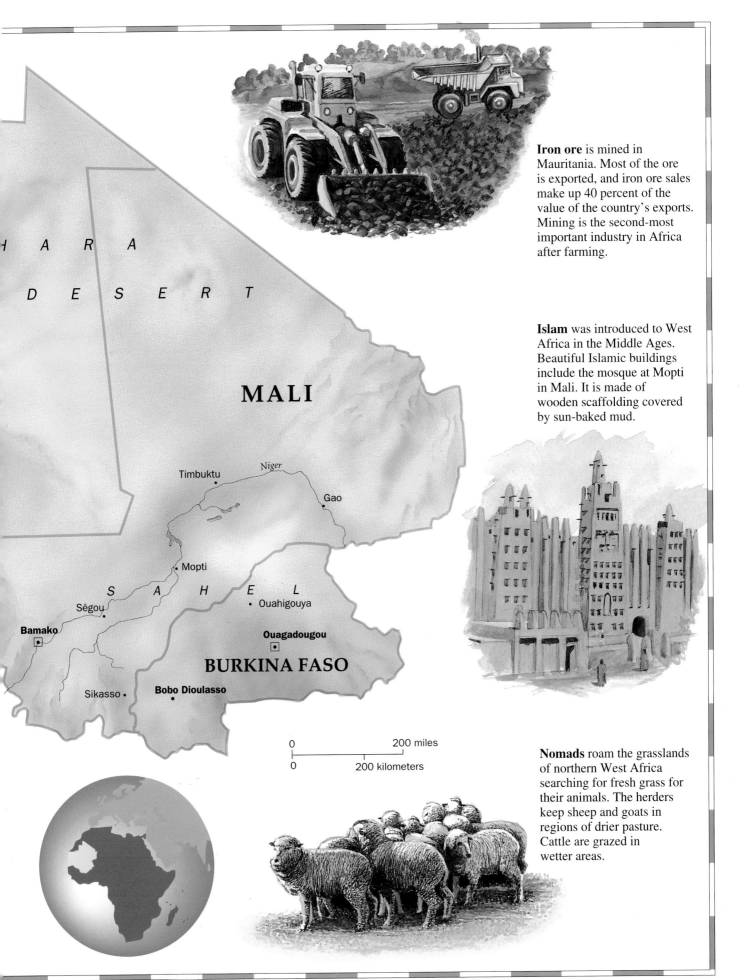

Iron ore is mined in Mauritania. Most of the ore is exported, and iron ore sales make up 40 percent of the value of the country's exports. Mining is the second-most important industry in Africa after farming.

Islam was introduced to West Africa in the Middle Ages. Beautiful Islamic buildings include the mosque at Mopti in Mali. It is made of wooden scaffolding covered by sun-baked mud.

SAHARA DESERT

MALI

Timbuktu

Niger

Gao

Mopti

SAHEL

Ségou

Ouahigouya

Bamako

Ouagadougou

BURKINA FASO

Sikasso

Bobo Dioulasso

| 0 | | 200 miles |
| 0 | | 200 kilometers |

Nomads roam the grasslands of northern West Africa searching for fresh grass for their animals. The herders keep sheep and goats in regions of drier pasture. Cattle are grazed in wetter areas.

WEST AFRICA 2

The part of West Africa shown here includes four mainland countries and Cape Verde, a group of islands in the Atlantic Ocean, 400 miles (640 km) west of Dakar. Liberia was founded by Americans in 1822 as a home for freed slaves and became independent in 1847. Guinea was ruled by France until 1958, Sierra Leone by Britain until 1961. Guinea-Bissau and Cape Verde were ruled by Portugal until the mid-1970s.

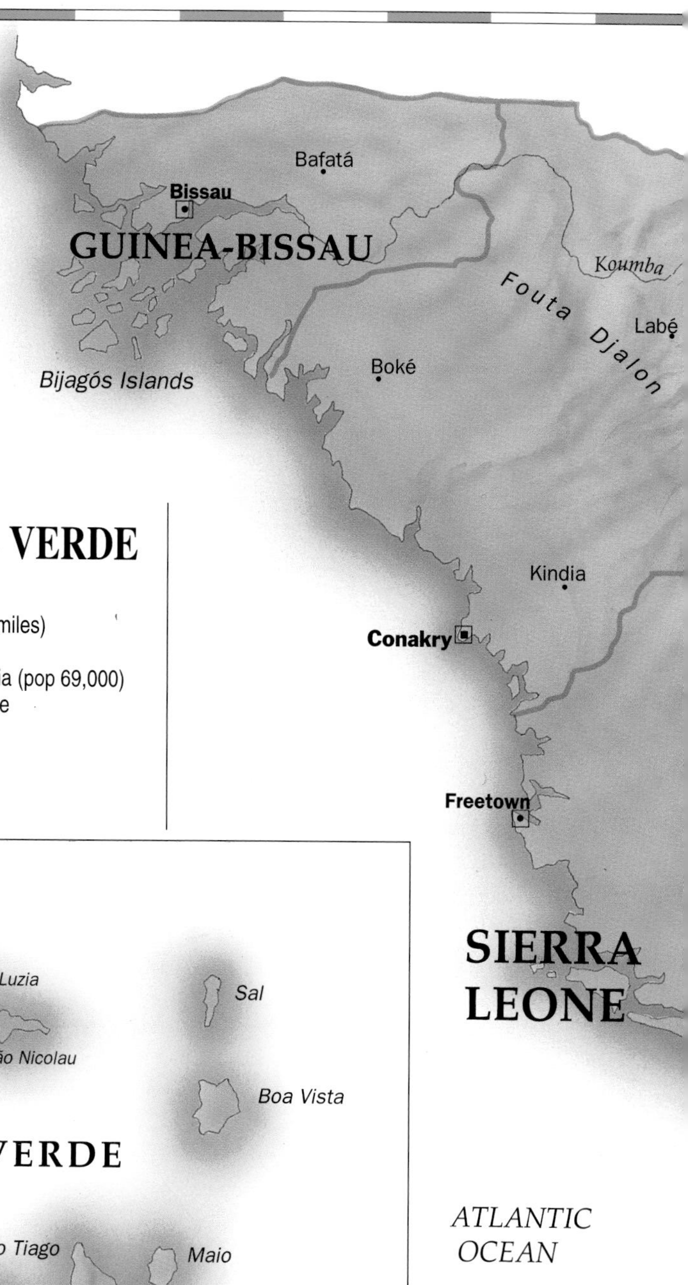

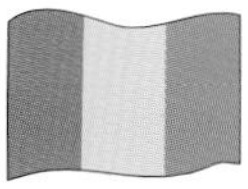

GUINEA

Area: 245,857 sq km (94,926 sq miles)
Population: 6,759,000
Capital and largest city: Conakry (pop 1,508,000)
Official language: French
Religions: Islam 87%, traditional religions 5%, Christian 8%
Government: Republic
Currency: Guinean franc

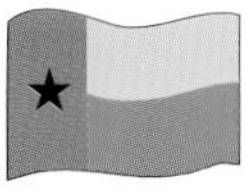

GUINEA-BISSAU

Area: 36,125 sq km (13,948 sq miles)
Population: 1,094,000
Capital and largest city: Bissau (pop 145,000)
Official language: Portuguese
Religions: traditional religions 54%, Islam 38%, Christianity 8%
Government: Republic
Currency: CFA franc

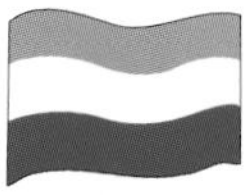

SIERRA LEONE

Area: 71,740 sq km (27,699 sq miles)
Population: 4,630,000
Capital and largest city: Freetown (pop 505,000)
Official language: English
Religions: Islam 60%, traditional religions 30%, Christianity 10%
Government: Republic
Currency: Leone

LIBERIA

Area: 111,369 sq km (43,000 sq miles)
Population: 2,810,000
Capital and largest city: Monrovia (pop 490,000)
Official language: English
Religions: Traditional religions 63%, Christianity 21%, Islam 16%
Government: Republic
Currency: Liberian dollar

CAPE VERDE

Area: 4,033 sq km (1,557 sq miles)
Population: 389,000
Capital and largest city: Praia (pop 69,000)
Official language: Portuguese
Religion: Christianity
Government: Republic
Currency: Escudo

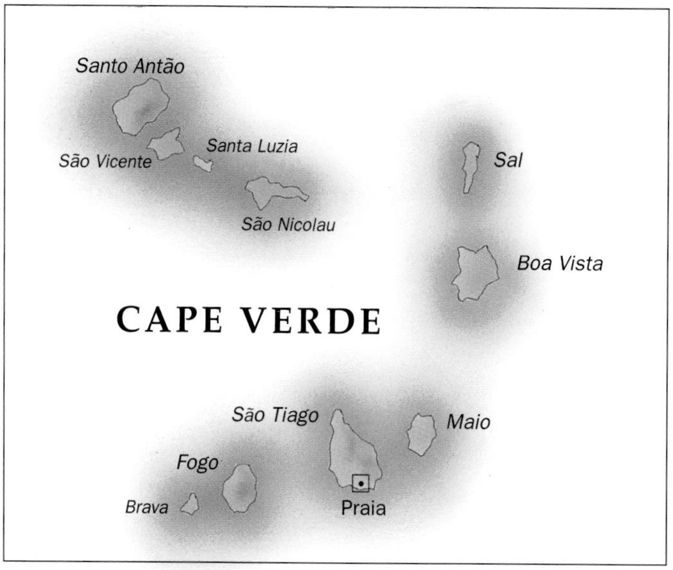

Bafatá

Bissau

GUINEA-BISSAU

Koumba

Fouta Djalon

Labé

Bijagós Islands

Boké

Kindia

Conakry

Freetown

SIERRA LEONE

Santo Antão

São Vicente

Santa Luzia

Sal

São Nicolau

Boa Vista

CAPE VERDE

São Tiago

Maio

Fogo

Brava

Praia

ATLANTIC OCEAN

0   100 miles
0   100 kilometers

Shrimp fishing is important in Guinea-Bissau, where shrimps make up about one-third of the country's exports. Groundnuts and coconuts make up another two-fifths of the exports.

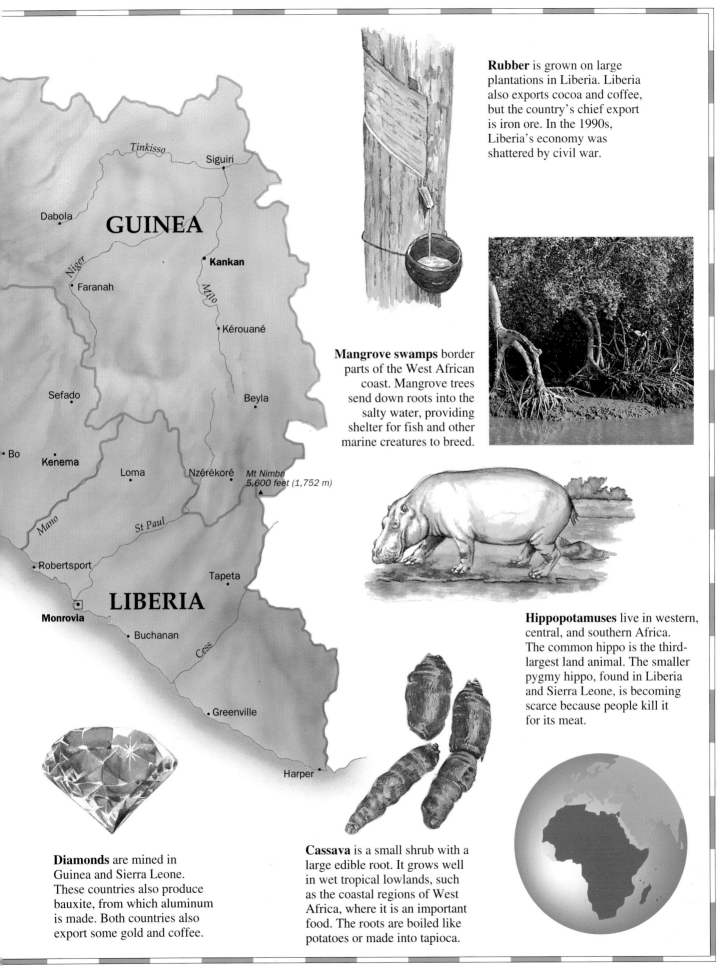

Rubber is grown on large plantations in Liberia. Liberia also exports cocoa and coffee, but the country's chief export is iron ore. In the 1990s, Liberia's economy was shattered by civil war.

Mangrove swamps border parts of the West African coast. Mangrove trees send down roots into the salty water, providing shelter for fish and other marine creatures to breed.

Hippopotamuses live in western, central, and southern Africa. The common hippo is the third-largest land animal. The smaller pygmy hippo, found in Liberia and Sierra Leone, is becoming scarce because people kill it for its meat.

Diamonds are mined in Guinea and Sierra Leone. These countries also produce bauxite, from which aluminum is made. Both countries also export some gold and coffee.

Cassava is a small shrub with a large edible root. It grows well in wet tropical lowlands, such as the coastal regions of West Africa, where it is an important food. The roots are boiled like potatoes or made into tapioca.

GUINEA

LIBERIA

Tinkisso
Siguiri
Dabola
Niger
Kankan
Faranah
Milo
Kérouané
Sefado
Beyla
Bo
Kenema
Loma
Nzérékoré
Mt Nimba
5,600 feet (1,752 m)
Mano
St Paul
Robertsport
Tapeta
Monrovia
Buchanan
Cess
Greenville
Harper

WEST AFRICA 3

Five countries make up the eastern part of West Africa. One of them, Nigeria, has more people than any other African country. Nigeria and Ghana were formerly British territories, while Benin, Ivory Coast, and Togo were ruled by France. Nearly half of the people in this part of West Africa earn their living by farming. Cocoa, coconuts, palm products, coffee, and cotton are leading exports. Nigeria's main export is oil.

Cocoa beans, from which chocolate is made, are grown in West Africa. The Ivory Coast and Ghana are the world's leading producers, while Nigeria ranks sixth. Other major products include coffee, cotton, palm oil, and palm kernels.

IVORY COAST

Area: 322,463 sq km (124,504 sq miles)
Population: 14,347,000
Capital: Yamoussoukro (pop 107,000)
Largest city: Abidjan (2,500,000)
Official language: French
Religions: Islam 39%, Christianity 26%, traditional religions 17%, other 18%
Government: Republic
Currency: CFA franc

GHANA

Area: 238,537 sq km (92,100 sq miles)
Population: 17,522,000
Capital and largest city: Accra (pop 1,781,000)
Official language: English
Religions: traditional religions 38%, Islam 30% Christianity 24%, other 8%
Government: Republic
Currency: Cedi

TOGO

Area: 56,785 sq km (21,925 sq miles)
Population: 4,230,000
Capital and largest city: Lomé (pop 590,000)
Official language: French
Religions: traditional religions 50%, Christianity 35%, Islam 15%
Government: Republic
Currency: CFA franc

BENIN

Area: 112,622 sq km (43,484 sq miles)
Population: 5,632,000
Capital: Porto-Novo (pop 179,000)
Largest city: Cotonou (537,000)
Official language: French
Religions: traditional religions 62%, Christianity 23%, Islam 12%, other 3%
Government: Republic
Currency: CFA franc

NIGERIA

Area: 923,768 sq km (356,669 sq miles)
Population: 114,568,000
Capital: Abuja (pop 339,000)
Largest city: Lagos (10,287,000)
Official language: English
Religions: Islam (51%), Christianity (40%), traditional religions (9%)
Government: Republic
Currency: Naira

ATLANTIC OCEAN

Yamoussoukro, capital of The Ivory Coast, has the world's largest church, the Basilica of Our Lady of Peace, which was completed in 1989. The city was the birthplace of Félix Houphouët-Boigny (1905-93), who was the country's president from 1960 to 1993.

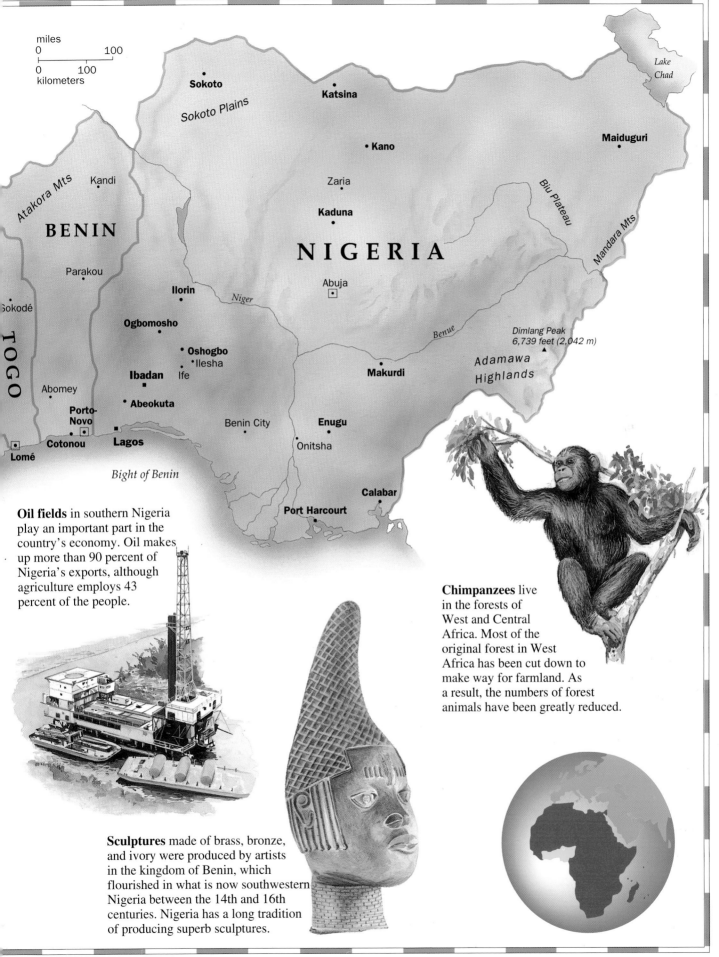

miles
0 100
0 100
kilometers

Sokoto

Katsina

Lake Chad

Maiduguri

Sokoto Plains

Kano

Atakora Mts

Kandi

Zaria

Kaduna

Biu Plateau

BENIN

NIGERIA

Mandara Mts

Parakou

Abuja

Ilorin

Niger

TOGO

Sokodé

Ogbomosho

Benue

Dimlang Peak
6,739 feet (2,042 m)

Oshogbo
Ilesha

Ife

Ibadan

Makurdi

Adamawa Highlands

Abomey

Abeokuta

Porto-Novo

Benin City

Enugu

Cotonou

Lagos

Onitsha

Lomé

Bight of Benin

Calabar

Port Harcourt

Oil fields in southern Nigeria play an important part in the country's economy. Oil makes up more than 90 percent of Nigeria's exports, although agriculture employs 43 percent of the people.

Chimpanzees live in the forests of West and Central Africa. Most of the original forest in West Africa has been cut down to make way for farmland. As a result, the numbers of forest animals have been greatly reduced.

Sculptures made of brass, bronze, and ivory were produced by artists in the kingdom of Benin, which flourished in what is now southwestern Nigeria between the 14th and 16th centuries. Nigeria has a long tradition of producing superb sculptures.

WEST-CENTRAL AFRICA

Bordering Nigeria are two huge landlocked nations, Chad and Niger. Although Niger has some mineral resources, these two countries are among the world's poorest. Both contain large areas of desert and dry grassland, and crops are grown only in the south. The Central African Republic, another landlocked country south of Chad, has grasslands in the north and forests in the south. Agriculture employs 86 percent of the people in this region.

NIGER

Area: 1,267,000 sq km (489,191 sq miles)
Population: 9,335,000
Capital: Niamey (pop 398,000)
Official language: French
Religions: Islam 89%, traditional religions 11%
Government: Republic
Currency: CFA franc

CHAD

Area: 1,284,000 sq km (495,755 sq miles)
Population: 6,611,000
Capital: N'Djamena (pop 530,000)
Official language: French
Religions: Islam 54%, Christianity 35%, traditional religions 7%, other 4%
Government: Republic
Currency: CFA franc

CENTRAL AFRICAN REPUBLIC

Area: 622,984 sq km (240,535 sq miles)
Population: 3,344,000
Capital: Bangui (pop 706,000)
Official language: French
Religions: traditional religions 57%, Christianity 35%, Islam 8%
Government: Republic
Currency: CFA franc

SAHARA

Air Mts

NIGER

Agadez

S

Niger

Tahoua

Maradi • Zinder

⦿ **Niamey**

Deserts cover most of northern Chad and Niger. To the south, the deserts merge into the dry, grassy Sahel. When severe droughts occur, the Sahel becomes desert. When the rains return, the Sahel becomes green again.

Lake Chad lies mainly in Chad, though parts of it are in Niger, Nigeria, and Cameroon. Its area changes regularly because the amount of rainfall in west-central Africa varies from year to year. The lake is rich in fish. It is also a source of salt and potash.

Niger was named after the Niger, one of Africa's longest rivers, which flows through southwestern Niger. Its waters are used to irrigate farmland. Southern Niger and Chad are covered by savanna.

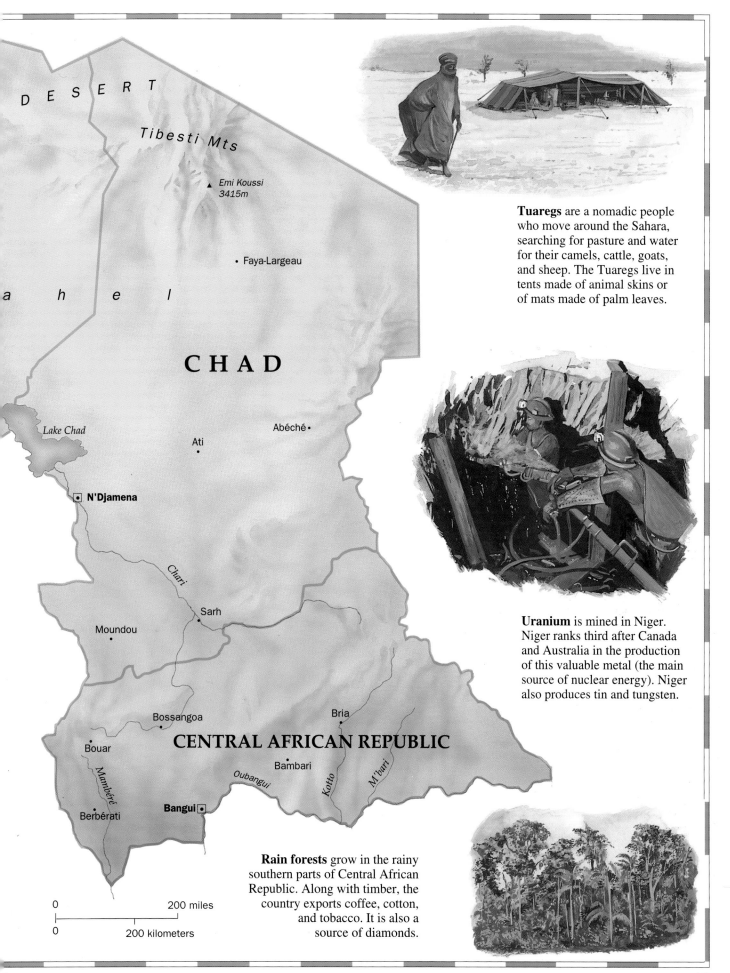

D E S E R T

Tibesti Mts

▲ Emi Koussi
3415m

a h e l

• Faya-Largeau

C H A D

Lake Chad

Abéché •

Ati •

☐ **N'Djamena**

Chari

• Sarh

Moundou •

Bossangoa •

CENTRAL AFRICAN REPUBLIC

Bouar •

Bambari •

Bria •

Oubangui

Kotto

M'bari

Membéré

Bangui ☐

Berbérati •

0 _____ 200 miles

0 _____ 200 kilometers

Tuaregs are a nomadic people who move around the Sahara, searching for pasture and water for their camels, cattle, goats, and sheep. The Tuaregs live in tents made of animal skins or of mats made of palm leaves.

Uranium is mined in Niger. Niger ranks third after Canada and Australia in the production of this valuable metal (the main source of nuclear energy). Niger also produces tin and tungsten.

Rain forests grow in the rainy southern parts of Central African Republic. Along with timber, the country exports coffee, cotton, and tobacco. It is also a source of diamonds.

19

CENTRAL AFRICA 1

Four tropical countries—Cameroon, Republic of Congo, Equatorial Guinea, and Gabon—lie between Nigeria and the huge Democratic Republic of Congo. Equatorial Guinea contains an area on the mainland and a volcanic island, Bioko, which contains its capital. South of Bioko lies the island nation of São Tomé and Príncipe. Most people in these countries work on farms. Congo and Gabon have important oil deposits.

CAMEROON

Area: 475,442 sq km (183,569 sq miles)
Population: 13,676,000
Capital: Yaoundé (pop 649,000)
Official language: English, French
Religions: Christianity 52%, traditional religions 26%, Islam 22%
Government: Republic
Currency: CFA franc

CONGO, REPUBLIC OF

Area: 342,000 sq km (132,047 sq miles)
Population: 2,705,000
Capital: Brazzaville (pop 938,000)
Official language: French
Religions: Christianity 65%, traditional religions 33%, Islam 2%,
Government: Republic
Currency: CFA franc

EQUATORIAL GUINEA

Area: 28,051 sq km (10,831 sq miles)
Population: 410,000
Capital: Malabo (pop 35,000)
Official language: Spanish, French
Religions: Christianity 89%, traditional religions 5%, other 6%
Government: Republic
Currency: CFA franc

GABON

Area: 267,667 sq km (103,347 sq miles)
Population: 1,125,000
Capital: Libreville (pop 418,000)
Official language: French
Religions: Christianity 80%, traditional religions 19%, Islam 1%,
Government: Republic
Currency: CFA franc

Soccer is a popular sport throughout Africa. National teams from Africa that have made their mark in international soccer competitions include Cameroon, Nigeria, and Morocco.

Plantains are a large kind of banana. They are grown throughout West and Central Africa, where they are eaten as a vegetable. The leaves are used to make bags or mats and sometimes for roofing houses.

ATLANTIC OCEAN

SÃO TOMÉ AND PRINCIPE

São Tomé
São Tomé

Annobón (Equat. Gui)

SÃO TOMÉ AND PRINCIPE

Area: 964 sq km (372 sq miles)
Population: 135,000
Capital: São Tomé (pop 43,000)
Official language: Portuguese
Religion: Christianity
Government: Republic
Currency: Dobra

Libreville, capital of Gabon, is a major port. Its name means "free town," and its origins are similar to those of Liberia. Libreville was founded by French officers in 1849 as a home for freed slaves.

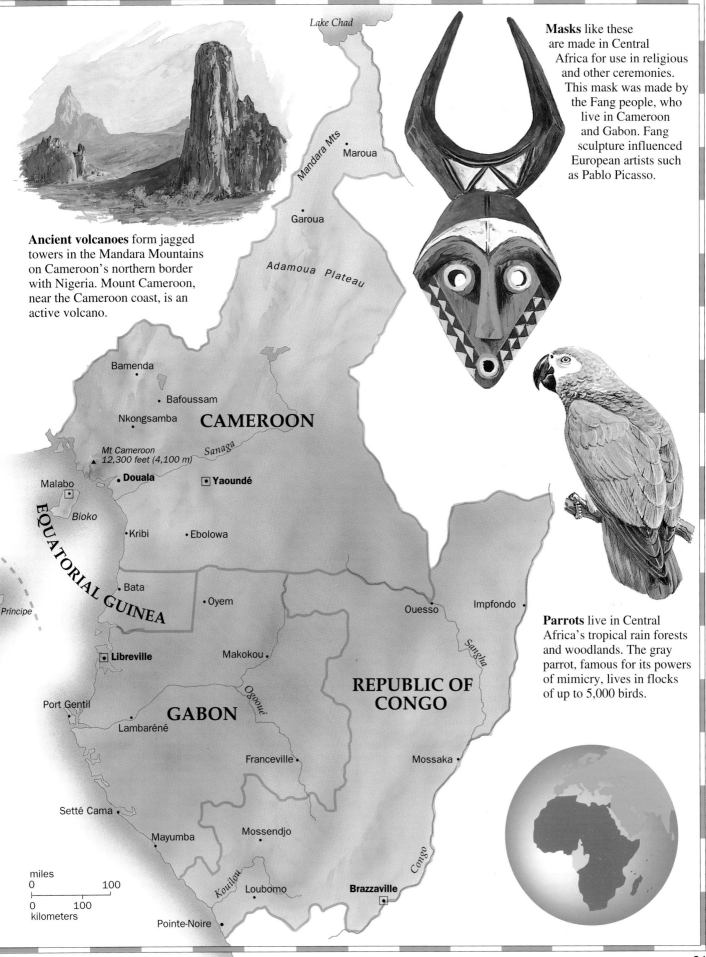

Lake Chad

Mandara Mts

Maroua

Masks like these are made in Central Africa for use in religious and other ceremonies. This mask was made by the Fang people, who live in Cameroon and Gabon. Fang sculpture influenced European artists such as Pablo Picasso.

Garoua

Ancient volcanoes form jagged towers in the Mandara Mountains on Cameroon's northern border with Nigeria. Mount Cameroon, near the Cameroon coast, is an active volcano.

Adamoua Plateau

Bamenda

Bafoussam

Nkongsamba **CAMEROON**

Sanaga

▲ Mt Cameroon
12,300 feet (4,100 m)

Malabo ☐ **Douala** ☐ **Yaoundé**

Bioko

EQUATORIAL GUINEA

Kribi Ebolowa

Príncipe

Bata Oyem

Ouesso Impfondo

Sangha

Libreville Makokou

Parrots live in Central Africa's tropical rain forests and woodlands. The gray parrot, famous for its powers of mimicry, lives in flocks of up to 5,000 birds.

Port Gentil

GABON

Ogooué

REPUBLIC OF CONGO

Lambaréné

Franceville Mossaka

Setté Cama

Mayumba Mossendjo

Kouilou

Congo

miles
0   100
0   100
kilometers

Loubomo **Brazzaville** ☐

Pointe-Noire

CENTRAL AFRICA 2

The Democratic Republic of Congo, called Zaire from 1971 to 1997, is Africa's third-largest country after Sudan and Algeria. It was ruled by Belgium until 1960, when the country was plunged into civil war between rival ethnic groups. The army leader General Joseph Mobutu (1930-97) restored order, but he became a dictator. Mobutu was overthrown in 1997. Burundi and Rwanda have also suffered brutal civil wars between two ethnic groups, the Hutus and Tutsis.

DEMOCRATIC REPUBLIC OF CONGO

Area: 2,345,409 sq km (905,568 sq miles)
Population: 45,234,000
Capital and largest cities:
Kinshasa (pop 4,655,000)
Other large cities:
Lubumbashi (851,000)
Mbuji Mayi (806,000)
Official language: French
Religions: Christianity 87%, traditional religions 12%, Islam 1%
Government: Military regime
Currency: Congo franc

BURUNDI

Area: 27,834 sq km (10,747 sq miles)
Population: 6,423,000
Capital: Bujumbura (pop 235,000)
Official languages: Rundi, French
Government: Republic (military regime)
Currency: Burundi franc

RWANDA

Area: 26,338 sq km (10,169 sq miles)
Population: 6,727,000
Capital: Kigali (pop 232,000)
Official languages: Kinyarwanda, French
Government: Republic
Currency: Rwanda franc

DEMOCRATIC REPUBLIC OF CONGO

Boma
Oubangui
Congo
Lisala
• Buta
Kisangani
• Mbandaka
Boende
Lomami
Inongo •
Bandundu
Kasai
Sankuru
• Ilebo
Kikwit
Lulua
Kananga
Kuango
• Mbuji Mayi
Kamina

ATLANTIC OCEAN
Boma
Congo
• Matadi
◻ Kinshasa

Laurent Kabila led the army that overthrew General Mobutu in 1997. He changed the country's name from Zaire to Democratic Republic of Congo. Kabila was assassinated in 2001.

0 — 200 miles
0 — 200 kilometers

Congo is also the name of the world's fifth-longest river. Called the Zaire from 1971 to 1997, the river has more water than any other besides the Amazon in South America. It is a major route for carrying goods through the dense rain forest.

Pygmies live in small groups in the forests of Central Africa. Sina around 100 BC, people from the Cameroon area, who spoke Bantu languages, began to settle in Central Africa. They pushed the Pygmies into remote areas. Bantu-speaking people now occupy most of Central, East, and Southern Africa.

Mountain gorillas live in Rwanda and in the mountains to the west. Their survival in Rwanda was threatened in the 1990s by fighting in the area where they live. Conflict between Hutus and Tutsis caused great loss of life and harmed the economies of Burundi and Rwanda.

Mining is a major industry in the Democratic Republic of Congo, which leads the world in mining industrial diamonds. It also produces copper, cobalt, manganese, silver, and tin. Some oil is obtained off the coast.

Coffee dominates the exports of both Burundi and Rwanda. The two war-shattered countries rank among the ten poorest in the world. Manufacturing and mining are on a small scale.

Isiro

Aruwimi

Lake Albert

Margherita Peak
15,330 feet
(5,110 m)

Lake Edward

RWANDA

Lake Kivu

Kigali

Bukavu

Bujumbura

BURUNDI

• Kindu

Lualaba

M i t u m b a   M t s

Lake Tanganyika

Kabalo

Kalemie

Lake Mweru

Katanga

Likasi

Kolwezi

Lubumbashi

EAST AFRICA

East Africa consists of three countries that were formerly ruled by Great Britain. Although the region lies on the equator, much of it is high plateaus where the weather is much more pleasant than on the hot and humid coast. All three countries have large national parks, where visitors can see a wide variety of wildlife at close range. More than 80 percent of the people live by farming. The main products include coffee, cotton, and tea.

UGANDA

Area: 236,036 sq km (91,134 sq miles)
Population: 19,741,000
Capital: Kampala (pop 874,000)
Official languages: Swahili, English
Religions: Christianity 65%, traditional religions 19%, Islam 15%, other 1%
Government: Republic
Currency: Uganda shilling

KENYA

Area: 582,646 sq km (224,961 sq miles)
Population: 27,364,000
Capital: Nairobi (pop 1,505,000)
Official languages: Swahili, English
Religions: Christianity 73%, traditional religions 19%, Islam 6%, other 2%
Government: Republic
Currency: Kenyan shilling

TANZANIA

Area: 945,087 sq km (364,900 sq miles)
Population: 30,494,000
Capital: Dodoma (pop 204,000)
Official languages: Swahili, English
Religions: Islam 35%, traditional religions 35%, Christianity 30%
Government: Republic
Currency: Tanzania shilling

Lake Victoria is Africa's largest lake and also the world's second-largest freshwater lake after Lake Superior in North America. One of the main sources of the Nile River, it was named after Queen Victoria.

Kilimanjaro, in northern Tanzania, is Africa's highest mountain. It is an extinct volcano. Early European explorers were amazed to find a mountain capped by ice and snow so close to the equator.

Serengeti National Park, in northern Tanzania, covers 14,500sq km (5,600 sq miles). It contains many animals, such as zebras, water buffaloes, elephants, gazelles, giraffes, leopards, and lions. Many tourists visit East Africa to see the wonderful wildlife.

Olduvai Gorge is a site in northern Tanzania where the fossils of ancient human-like creatures have been found, together with the tools they used. Many scientists believe that the first true humans evolved in East Africa.

Masai herders live in Kenya and Tanzania. Kenya is home to about 40 different ethnic groups, and Tanzania is home to 120. Each group has its own language, but most speak a second language, Swahili, so they can talk to people from other groups.

Gulu

Nile

Masindi

Lake Albert

Kabarole

Entebbe

Lake Edward

Bukoba

Ujiji

Lake Tanganyika

Lake Rukwa

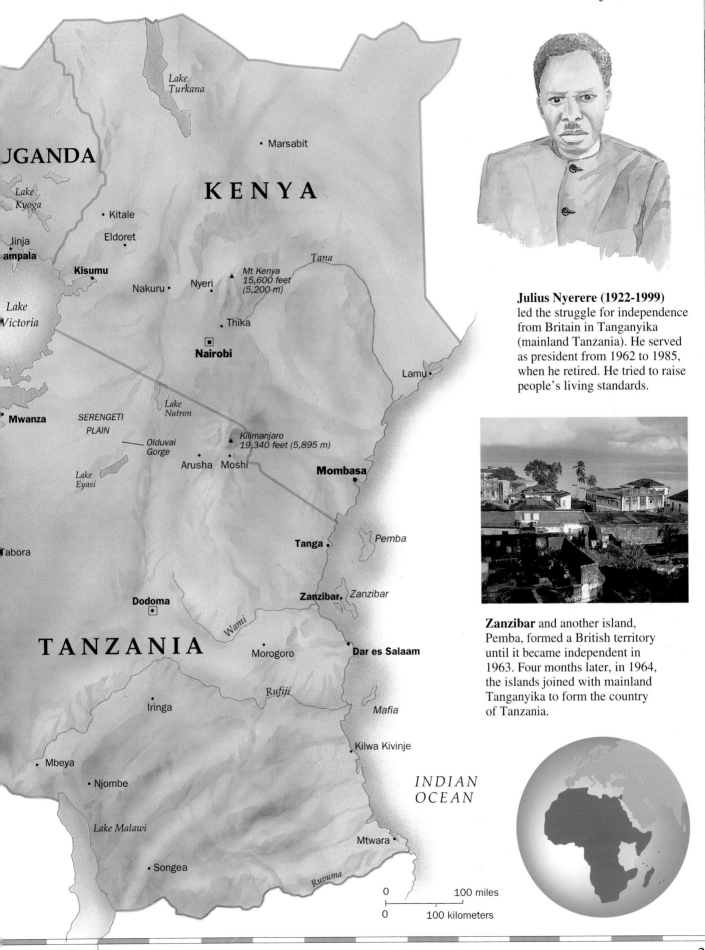

UGANDA

KENYA

Lake Turkana

• Marsabit

Lake Kyoga

Jinja

ampala

• Kitale

Eldoret

Kisumu

Nakuru • • Nyeri

▲ Mt Kenya
15,600 feet
(5,200 m)

Tana

Lake Victoria

• Thika

☐ **Nairobi**

Lamu •

Mwanza

SERENGETI PLAIN

Lake Natron

Olduvai Gorge

▲ Kilimanjaro
19,340 feet (5,895 m)

Arusha • • Moshi

Mombasa

Lake Eyasi

Tabora

Pemba

Tanga •

Dodoma
☐

Wami

Zanzibar • *Zanzibar*

TANZANIA

Morogoro •

Dar es Salaam

Rufiji

• Iringa

Mafia

• Kilwa Kivinje

• Mbeya

• Njombe

INDIAN OCEAN

Lake Malawi

Mtwara •

• Songea

Ruvuma

0   100 miles

0   100 kilometers

Julius Nyerere (1922-1999)
led the struggle for independence
from Britain in Tanganyika
(mainland Tanzania). He served
as president from 1962 to 1985,
when he retired. He tried to raise
people's living standards.

Zanzibar and another island,
Pemba, formed a British territory
until it became independent in
1963. Four months later, in 1964,
the islands joined with mainland
Tanganyika to form the country
of Tanzania.

25

INDIAN OCEAN TERRITORIES

Four independent island countries in the Indian Ocean are considered to be part of the African continent. They are Madagascar, which is by far the largest, the Comoros, Mauritius, and the Seychelles. The French island of Réunion, east of Madagascar, is also part of Africa. Madagascar is unusual. Its people are of mixed Indonesian and black African descent. Its chief language, Malagasy, resembles Malay and Indonesian.

 **SEYCHELLES**

Area: 404 sq km (156 sq miles)
Population: 77,000
Capital: Victoria (pop 30,000)
Official language: None
Religions: Christianity 96%, Hinduism 1%, other 3%
Government: Republic
Currency: Seychelles rupee

 **COMOROS**

Area: 2,171 sq km (838 sq miles)
Population: 505,000
Capital: Moroni (pop 22,000)
Official languages: Comorian, Arabic, French
Religions: Islam 99%, Christianity 1%
Government: Islamic republic
Currency: Comorian franc

 **MADAGASCAR**

Area: 587,041 sq km (226,658 sq miles)
Population: 13,705,000
Capital: Antananarivo (pop 1,053,000)
Official language: Malagasy
Religions: traditional religions 52%, Christianity 41%, Islam 7%
Government: Republic
Currency: Malagasy franc

 **MAURITIUS**

Area: 1,865 sq km (720 sq miles)
Population: 1,134,000
Capital: Port Louis (pop 146,000)
Official language: English
Religions: Hinduism 51%, Christianity 32%, Islam 16%, other 1%
Government: Republic
Currency: Mauritian rupee

Lemurs, a name meaning "ghosts," are primates that live on Madagascar and the Comoros. They evolved over the last 60 million years, when the islands were cut off from mainland Africa.

Spices are grown on Indian Ocean islands. The Comoros, a producer of cloves, vanilla and perfume oils, became independent in 1975. Two of the three islands tried to break away from the country in 1997-98.

RÉUNION
(French overseas department)

Area: 2,510 sq km (969 sq miles)
Population: 664,000
Capital: Saint-Denis (pop 104,000)
Official language: French
Religions: Christianity (94%), other (6%)
Currency: French franc

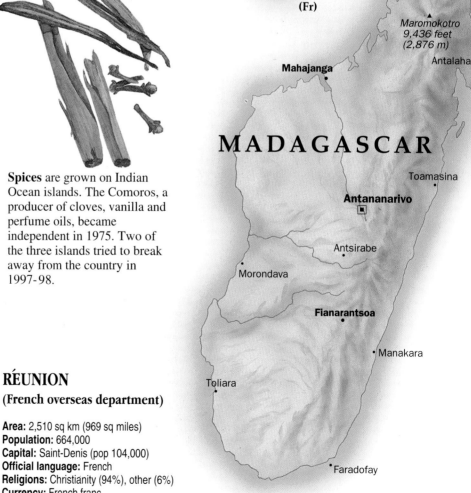

SEYCH...

Aldabra

Moroni

COMOROS

Dzaoudzi

MAYOTTE (Fr)

Antsiranana

Maromokotro 9,436 feet (2,876 m)

Antalaha

Mahajanga

MADAGASCAR

Toamasina

Antananarivo

Antsirabe

Morondava

Fianarantsoa

Manakara

Toliara

Faradofay

L L E S

☐ Victoria
Mahé

I N D I A N   O C E A N

```
0                    200 miles
|----|----|----|----|----|
0                    200 kilometers
```

Turtles, like this leatherback, come on shore in the Seychelles and other islands to lay their eggs. Hunted for food and for their shells, they are now an endangered species, although there are no reliable records of their numbers.

Tourism is essential to the economy of the Seychelles, which has many beautiful beaches. Tourism is also important on other islands, especially Mauritius and Madagascar.

Rice is the chief food crop in Madagascar. Historians believe that rice growing was introduced to Madagascar by people from southeast Asia who settled on the island. Coffee is Madagascar's leading export.

MAURITIUS

Port Louis ▣

Saint-Denis ▣

RÉUNION (Fr)

Sugarcane is the leading crop and one of the chief exports of Mauritius. Most of it is grown on large plantations. Sugar production employs about one-third of all workers on the island.

SOUTHEASTERN AFRICA

Southeastern Africa consists of two former British colonies—Malawi and Swaziland—and the former Portuguese colony of Mozambique. Malawi became independent in 1964 and Swaziland in 1968. Mozambique achieved independence in 1975. A civil war then occurred as a rebel force, supported by the white governments in Rhodesia (now Zimbabwe) and South Africa, fought to overthrow the new government. Although civil war in Mozambique officially ended in 1992 the fighting continued into the early years of the 21st century.

MALAWI

Area: 118,484 sq km (45,747 sq miles)
Population: 10,016,000
Capital: Lilongwe (pop 234,000)
Official languages: Chichewa, English
Religions: Christianity 50%, Islam 20%, traditional religions 10%, other 20%
Government: Republic
Currency: Kwacha

MOZAMBIQUE

Area: 801,590 sq km (309,496 sq miles)
Population: 18,028,000
Capital: Maputo (pop 934,000)
Official language: Portuguese
Religions: Traditional religions 48%, Christianity 39%, Islam 13%
Government: Republic
Currency: Metical

SWAZILAND

Area: 17,363 sq km (6,704 sq miles)
Population: 926,000
Capital: Mbabane (pop 38,000)
Official languages: Swazi, English
Religions: Christianity 77%, traditional religions 21%, other 2%
Government: Monarchy
Currency: Lilangeni

Hastings Kamuzu Banda (1898-1997) led the independence struggle in Malawi. After independence in 1964, he became prime minister and later president, suppressing all opposition. He was defeated in elections in 1994 and died in 1997.

Lake Malawi occupies part of the Great Rift Valley. This deep valley runs from southeastern Africa, through East Africa and Ethiopia to the Red Sea. It continues into southwestern Asia, where it contains the Dead Sea.

Hydroelectricity is produced at the Cabora Bassa Dam on the Zambezi River in western Mozambique. Coal and oil are in short supply in much of southern Africa. Hydroelectric plants are major sources of electricity.

Pineapples are an important crop in Swaziland, together with citrus fruits, cotton, rice, sugar-cane, and tobacco. Swaziland has a varied economy. It is one of the few countries in Africa that exports more than it imports.

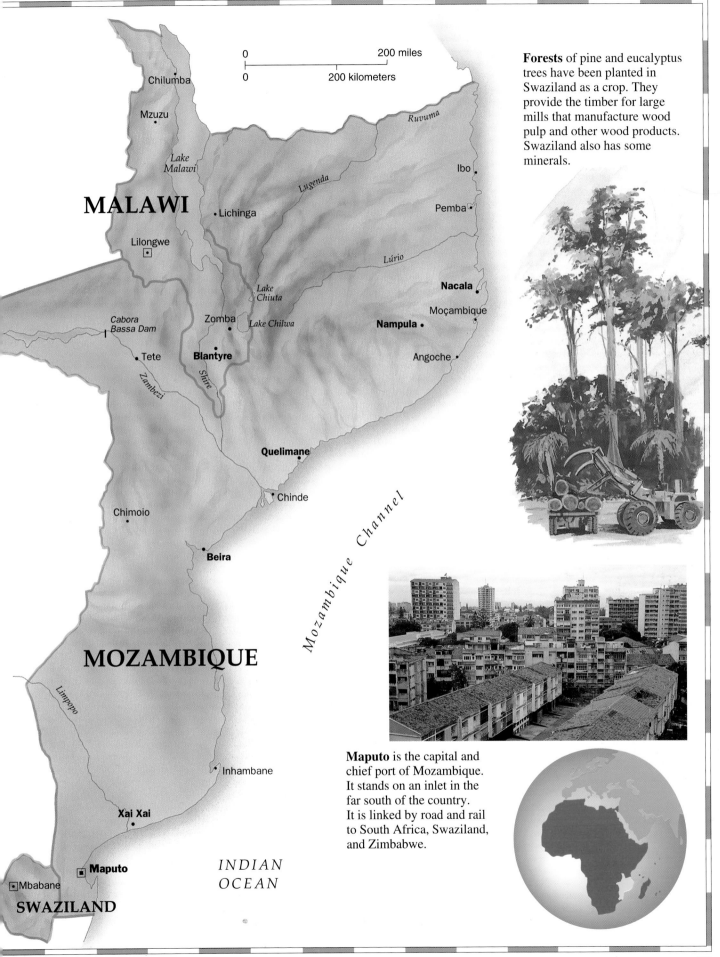

MALAWI

Chilumba

Mzuzu

Lake Malawi

Lilongwe

Lichinga

Ruvuma

Lugenda

Ibo

Pemba

Lúrio

Nacala

Lake Chiuta

Zomba

Lake Chilwa

Moçambique

Nampula

Cabora Bassa Dam

Tete

Blantyre

Shire

Zambezi

Angoche

Quelimane

Chinde

Chimoio

Beira

Mozambique Channel

MOZAMBIQUE

Limpopo

Inhambane

Xai Xai

Maputo

Mbabane

INDIAN OCEAN

SWAZILAND

0 — 200 miles
0 — 200 kilometers

Forests of pine and eucalyptus trees have been planted in Swaziland as a crop. They provide the timber for large mills that manufacture wood pulp and other wood products. Swaziland also has some minerals.

Maputo is the capital and chief port of Mozambique. It stands on an inlet in the far south of the country. It is linked by road and rail to South Africa, Swaziland, and Zimbabwe.

SOUTH-CENTRAL AFRICA

Two large landlocked countries—Zambia and Zimbabwe—lie at the heart of southern Africa. Zambia is a former British territory that was called Northern Rhodesia before it became independent in 1964. Zimbabwe is also a former British colony. Before achieving independence in 1980, it was known as Rhodesia. Both countries have important mineral resources, but agriculture still employs about 70 percent of the people.

Beef cattle are reared on large ranches in Zimbabwe. Dairy cattle are also important, and milk is a major product. Maize (corn) is the chief food crop in both Zimbabwe and Zambia.

ZAMBIA

Area: 752,614 sq km (290,586 sq miles)
Population: 9,215,000
Capital and largest cities:
Lusaka (pop 921,000)
Other large cities: Kitwe (495,000)
Ndola (467,000)
Kabwe (210,000)
Mufulira (206,000)
Official language: English
Religions: Christianity 72%, traditional religions 27%, other 1%
Government: Republic
Currency: Kwacha

ZIMBABWE

Area: 390,580 sq km (150,804 sq miles)
Population: 11,248,000
Capital and largest cities:
Harare (pop 1,184,000)
Other large cities: Bulawayo (621,000)
Chitungwiza (274,000)
Mutare (132,000)
Gweru (125,000)
Official language: English
Religions: Christianity 45%, traditional religions 40%, other 15%
Government: Republic
Currency: Zimbabwe dollar

Copper is mined in a region called the Copperbelt in northern Zambia, along the border with the Democratic Republic of Congo. Copper accounts for about 70 percent of Zambia's exports.

Great Zimbabwe is a historic site in Zimbabwe that contains the ruins of impressive stone buildings. It was capital of a Shona kingdom that flourished between the Limpopo and Zambezi rivers between about 1250 and 1450.

Tobacco is a major export of Zimbabwe. The country ranks sixth among the world's tobacco producers. Zimbabwe also exports corn and cotton. Zambia also produces some tobacco.

Kasempa •

• Mongu

Sesheke •

Livingstone •

Victoria Falls

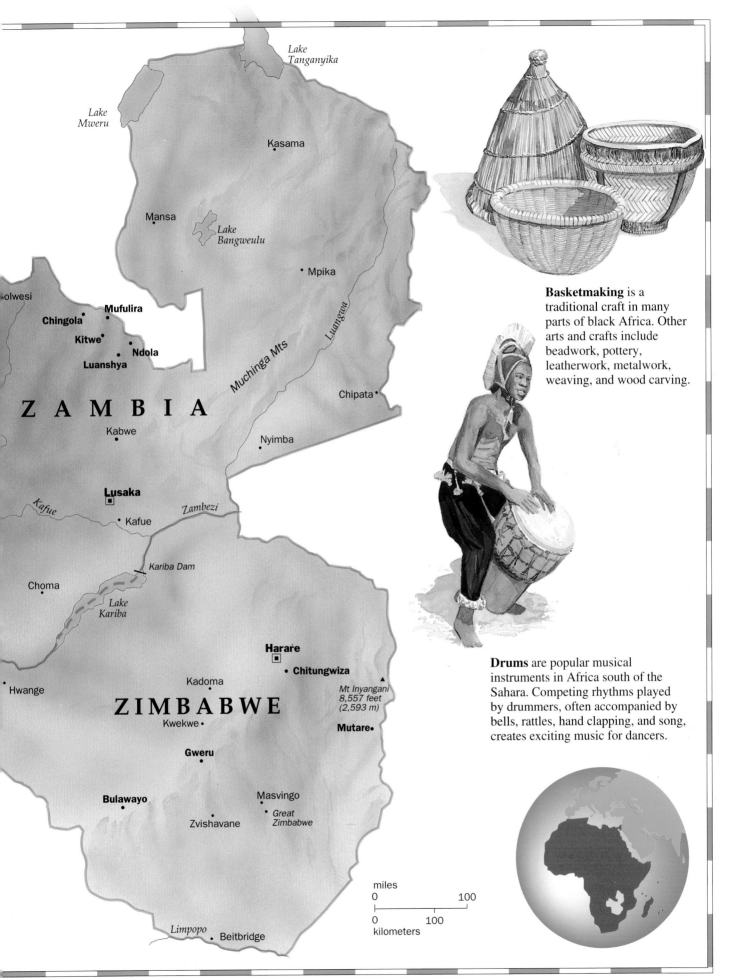

Lake
Tanganyika

Lake
Mweru

Kasama

Mansa

Lake
Bangweulu

Mpika

•olwesi

Mufulira

Chingola

Kitwe

Ndola

Luanshya

Luangwa

Muchinga Mts

Chipata •

Z A M B I A

Kabwe

Nyimba

Lusaka

Kafue

Zambezi

• Kafue

Kariba Dam

Choma

Lake
Kariba

Harare

• **Chitungwiza**

Kadoma

Mt Inyangani
8,557 feet
(2,593 m)

• Hwange

Z I M B A B W E

Kwekwe •

Mutare•

Gweru

Bulawayo

Masvingo

• Great
Zimbabwe

Zvishavane

Limpopo

Beitbridge

miles
0   100

0   100
kilometers

Basketmaking is a
traditional craft in many
parts of black Africa. Other
arts and crafts include
beadwork, pottery,
leatherwork, metalwork,
weaving, and wood carving.

Drums are popular musical
instruments in Africa south of the
Sahara. Competing rhythms played
by drummers, often accompanied by
bells, rattles, hand clapping, and song,
creates exciting music for dancers.

31

SOUTHWESTERN AFRICA

Southwestern Africa consists of Angola and Namibia, on the Atlantic Ocean coast, and Botswana, a landlocked country that borders Namibia. Botswana is a former British territory that became independent in 1966. Angola became independent from Portugal in 1975, but it then suffered a long civil war. Namibia, formerly called South West Africa, became independent from South Africa in 1990.

Maize (corn) is an important part of the diet of many black Africans in southern Africa. It contains starch, which provides the body with energy, but it lacks many other nutrients the body needs. People who depend on it exclusively may suffer from malnutrition.

ANGOLA

Area: 1,246,700 sq km (481,354 sq miles)
Population: 11,100,000
Capital: Luanda (pop 2,250,000)
Official language: Portuguese
Religions: Christianity 70%, traditional religions 30%
Government: Republic
Currency: Kwanza

NAMIBIA

Area: 824,292 sq km (318,261 sq miles)
Population: 1,584,000
Capital: Windhoek (pop 126,000)
Official language: English
Religions: Christianity 82%, other 18%
Government: Republic
Currency: Namibian dollar

BOTSWANA

Area: 581,730 sq km (224,607 sq miles)
Population: 1,480,000
Capital: Gaborone (pop 133,000)
Official languages: English, Setswana
Religioins: Christianity 50%, traditional religions 49%, other 1%
Government: Republic **Currency:** Pula

Wood carving is one of the leading art forms in black Africa. Carvings of chiefs and heroes by the Chokwe people of Angola, made over the last 200 years, are found in museums all throught the world. Because wood is perishable, few older carvings have survived.

Sand dunes form towering hills in the Namib Desert, which stretches along the western coast of Namibia. Most of the little water the desert receives comes from mists that roll in from the sea.

CABINDA
(Angola)
Cabinda

Luanda

Cuanza

Malanje

ANGOLA

Lobito

Serra Moco
8,643 feet (2,619 m)

Benguela

Huambo

Cubango

Namibe

Lubango

Cunene

Etosha Pan

N
a
m
i
b

Otjiwarongo

ATLANTIC OCEAN

NAMIBIA

Windhoek

Walvis Bay

D
e
s
e
r
t

Lüderitz

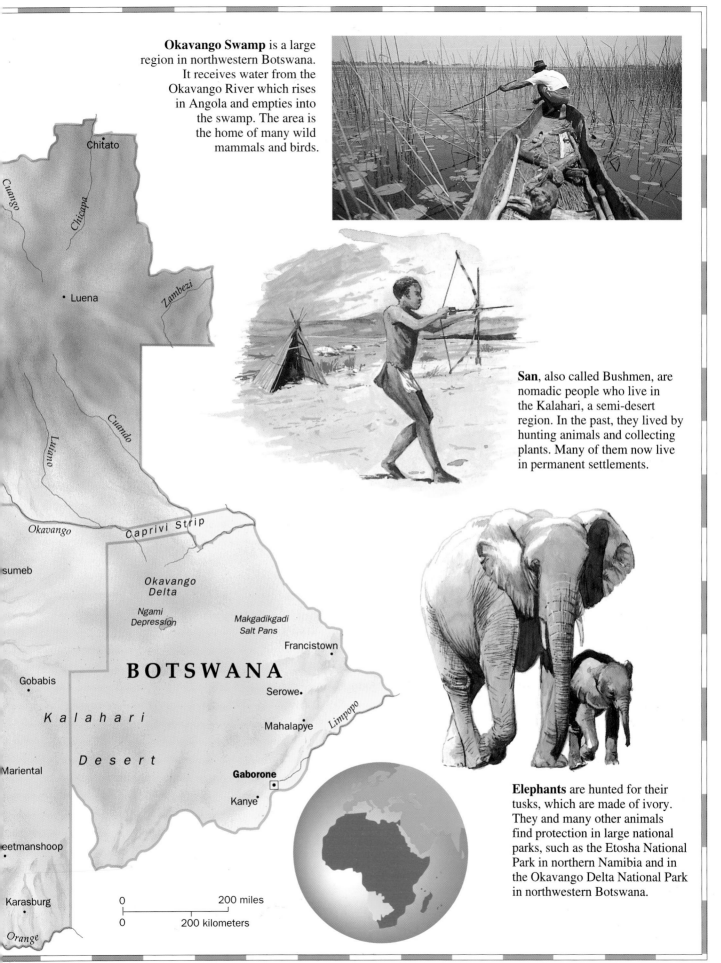

Okavango Swamp is a large region in northwestern Botswana. It receives water from the Okavango River which rises in Angola and empties into the swamp. The area is the home of many wild mammals and birds.

San, also called Bushmen, are nomadic people who live in the Kalahari, a semi-desert region. In the past, they lived by hunting animals and collecting plants. Many of them now live in permanent settlements.

Elephants are hunted for their tusks, which are made of ivory. They and many other animals find protection in large national parks, such as the Etosha National Park in northern Namibia and in the Okavango Delta National Park in northwestern Botswana.

Chitato

Cuango

Chicapa

Zambezi

• Luena

Cuando

Luiano

Okavango

Caprivi Strip

sumeb

Okavango Delta

Ngami Depression

Makgadikgadi Salt Pans

Francistown

BOTSWANA

Gobabis

Serowe•

Kalahari

Mahalapye

Limpopo

Desert

Mariental

Gaborone

Kanye•

eetmanshoop

Karasburg

Orange

0   200 miles

0   200 kilometers

SOUTHERN AFRICA

South Africa and Lesotho occupy the southern tip of Africa. South Africa is Africa's most developed country, though much of the population lives in poverty. In 1948, the South African government introduced a policy called apartheid, or legal separation of the races. Multiracial elections in 1994 produced a government and equal rights for all the people in South Africa.

Gold mining is an important industry in South Africa, which leads the world in gold production. The country also produces coal, chromite, copper, diamonds, iron ore, manganese, platinum, and uranium. South Africa is also the most industrialized country in Africa.

SOUTH AFRICA

Area: 1,221,037 sq km (471,445 sq miles)
Population: 37,643,000
Capitals: Pretoria (administrative),
Cape Town (legislative), Bloemfontein (judicial)
Largest cities: Cape Town (pop 2,350,000)
Johannesburg (1,196,000)
Durban (1,137,000)
Pretoria (1,080,000)
Port Elizabeth (853,000)
Official languages: Afrikaans, English,
Ndebele, North Sotho, South Sotho, Swazi,
Tsonga, Tswana, Venda, Xhosa, Zulu
Religions: Christianity 66%, traditional religions 30%, Hinduism 1%, Islam 1%, other 2%
Government: Republic
Currency: Rand

LESOTHO

Area: 30,355 sq km (11,720 sq miles)
Population: 2,023,000
Capital: Maseru (pop 109,000)
Official languages: Sesotho, English
Religions: Christianity 93%,
traditional religions 7%
Government: Monarchy
Currency: Loti

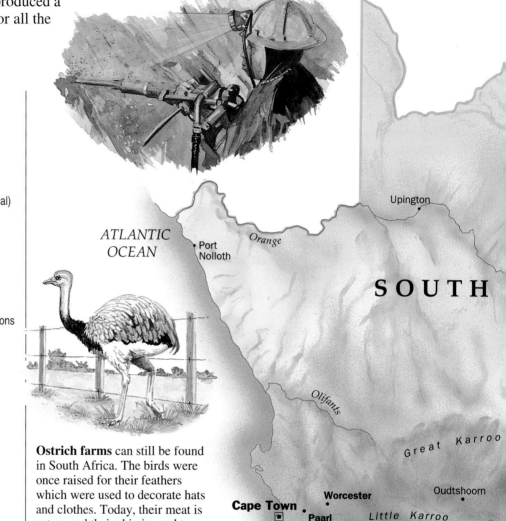

Ostrich farms can still be found in South Africa. The birds were once raised for their feathers which were used to decorate hats and clothes. Today, their meat is eaten, and their skin is used to make leather.

Table Mountain is a flat-topped elevated region that overlooks Cape Town and Table Bay, in southwestern South Africa. Clouds often cover the top of Table Mountain and spill over the edge like a tablecloth.

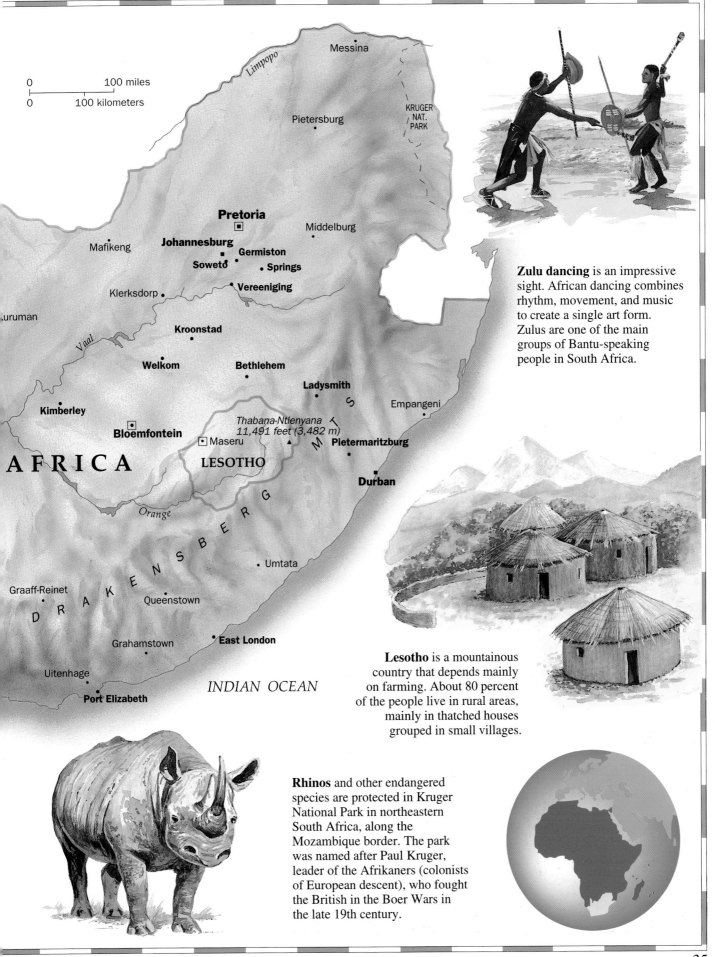

0 ⊢——————⊣ **100 miles**
0 ⊢——————⊣ **100 kilometers**

Limpopo

Messina

KRUGER
NAT.
PARK

Pietersburg

Pretoria
☐

Middelburg

Mafikeng

Johannesburg
Germiston
Soweto
Springs

Vereeniging

Klerksdorp

uruman

Vaal

Kroonstad

Welkom
Bethlehem

Ladysmith

Empangeni

Kimberley

Thabana-Ntlenyana
11,491 feet (3,482 m)
▲

Pietermaritzburg

Bloemfontein
☐ Maseru

A F R I C A
LESOTHO

M
T
S

Durban

Orange

D
R
A
K
E
N
S
B
E
R
G

• Umtata

Graaff-Reinet

Queenstown

Grahamstown
East London

Uitenhage

INDIAN OCEAN

Port Elizabeth

Zulu dancing is an impressive
sight. African dancing combines
rhythm, movement, and music
to create a single art form.
Zulus are one of the main
groups of Bantu-speaking
people in South Africa.

Lesotho is a mountainous
country that depends mainly
on farming. About 80 percent
of the people live in rural areas,
mainly in thatched houses
grouped in small villages.

Rhinos and other endangered
species are protected in Kruger
National Park in northeastern
South Africa, along the
Mozambique border. The park
was named after Paul Kruger,
leader of the Afrikaners (colonists
of European descent), who fought
the British in the Boer Wars in
the late 19th century.

PEOPLE AND BELIEFS

Africa is home to about 13 percent of the world's population. Huge areas are thinly populated, others are overcrowded. Densely populated areas include the Nile valley and northwest coast, parts of West Africa, the lakelands of East Africa, and southeastern Africa.

The Shona people of Zimbabwe traditionally used divining tablets like these to uncover secrets and tell the future.

Population densities in Africa

Number of people per square kilometer

- Over 100
- Between 50 and 100
- Between 10 and 50
- Between 1 and 10
- Below 1

Main cities

- ■ Cities of more than 1,000,000 people
- ● Cities of more than 500,000 people

Population and Area

Africa's largest countries are Sudan, Algeria, and the Democratic Republic of Congo. Sudan contains large, thinly populated deserts, swamps, and humid rain forests, while many people are concentrated in the Nile valley. Nigeria, the 13th-largest country, has the largest population in Africa. The most densely populated countries on the African mainland are Rwanda and Burundi. About one-third of Africa's people live in cities and towns. The largest city is Cairo.

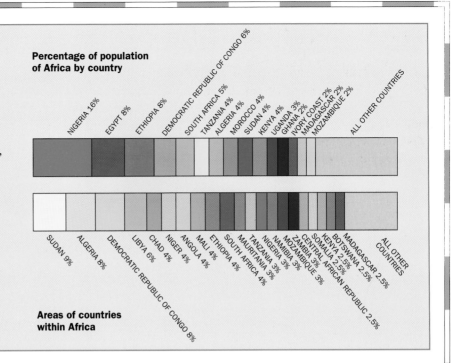

Percentage of population of Africa by country

NIGERIA 16% · EGYPT 8% · ETHIOPIA 8% · DEMOCRATIC REPUBLIC OF CONGO 6% · SOUTH AFRICA 5% · TANZANIA 4% · ALGERIA 4% · MOROCCO 4% · SUDAN 4% · KENYA 4% · UGANDA 3% · GHANA 2% · IVORY COAST 2% · MADAGASCAR 2% · MOZAMBIQUE 2% · ALL OTHER COUNTRIES

SUDAN 9% · ALGERIA 8% · DEMOCRATIC REPUBLIC OF CONGO 8% · LIBYA 6% · CHAD 4% · NIGER 4% · ANGOLA 4% · MALI 4% · ETHIOPIA 4% · SOUTH AFRICA 4% · MAURITANIA 4% · TANZANIA 3% · NIGERIA 3% · NAMIBIA 3% · MOZAMBIQUE 3% · ZAMBIA 3% · CENTRAL AFRICAN REPUBLIC 3% · SOMALIA 2.5% · KENYA 2.5% · BOTSWANA 2.5% · MADAGASCAR 2.5% · ALL OTHER COUNTRIES

Areas of countries within Africa

Main Religions

In the 7th century AD, Arabs migrated from the Arabia Peninsula across North Africa, converting people to Islam. In the Middle Ages, Islam spread south of the Sahara, especially into West and East Africa. Today, less than 40 percent of Africa's people are Muslims. The Ethiopian Christian Church has existed since the 4th century AD, but Christianity did not reach most of Africa south of the Sahara until the 19th century. Today, about 39 percent of the people of Africa are Christians. Most other Africans follow traditional religions.

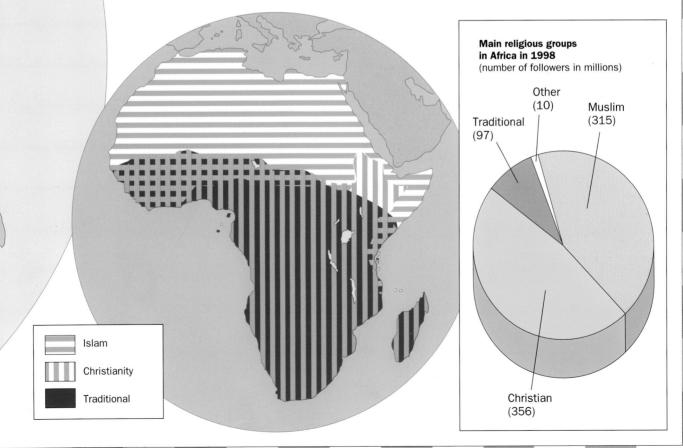

Islam

Christianity

Traditional

Main religious groups in Africa in 1998
(number of followers in millions)

Other (10)

Muslim (315)

Traditional (97)

Christian (356)

CLIMATE AND VEGETATION

Rain forests grow in the tropical rainy climatic region around the equator. Savanna (grassland with scattered trees) occurs in places with tropical climates with wet and dry seasons. The savanna regions merge into dry grasslands and deserts. Mediterranean climates, with hot, dry summers and mild, rainy winters, occur in the far northwest and southwest.

Only about one-third of Africa's land is used for farming, though more than half the people are farmers.

Legend:
- Mountain
- Broadleaf forest
- Prairie
- Steppe
- Savanna
- Mediterranean
- Dry tropical scrub
- Desert
- Tropical rain forest

Most of Africa has a tropical climate, but the height of the land affects temperatures. On the East African highlands, temperatures are much lower than on the hot and humid coast. The highlands have a pleasant climate throughout the year.

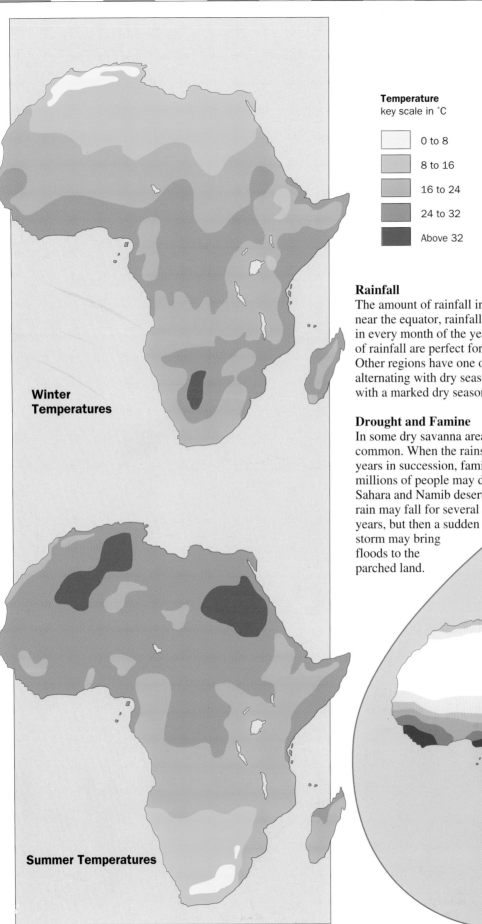

Temperature
key scale in °C

	0 to 8
	8 to 16
	16 to 24
	24 to 32
	Above 32

Winter Temperatures

Summer Temperatures

Range of climates

Most of Africa lies in the tropics, and so most of the continent has a tropical climate. Temperatures usually vary little between winter and summer. In many areas, the difference between day and night temperatures is often greater than the difference between summer and winter temperatures. The highest temperatures occur in the Sahara. The coolest regions are in the northwest and in parts of South Africa. Frost and snow occur on some tropical African mountains.

Rainfall

The amount of rainfall in Africa varies greatly. In regions near the equator, rainfall is heavy, and rain occurs in every month of the year. High temperatures and plenty of rainfall are perfect for the growth of dense rain forests. Other regions have one or two rainy seasons every year, alternating with dry seasons. Savanna is common in areas with a marked dry season.

Drought and Famine

In some dry savanna areas, droughts are common. When the rains fail for several years in succession, famine occurs and millions of people may die. In the Sahara and Namib deserts, no rain may fall for several years, but then a sudden storm may bring floods to the parched land.

Annual rainfall
in mm

	Above 3000
	2000 - 3000
	1000 - 2000
	500 - 1000
	250 - 500
	0 - 250

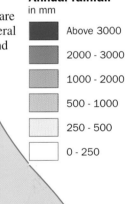

ECOLOGY AND ENVIRONMENT

By the end of the 20th century, Africa's population was increasing by about 2.6 percent per year—faster than any other continent. The rapid increase in population in the last 50 years has led to the destruction of forests and savanna, causing great damage to the land in many areas.

Mosquitoes spread malaria

Tsetse flies spread sleeping sickness

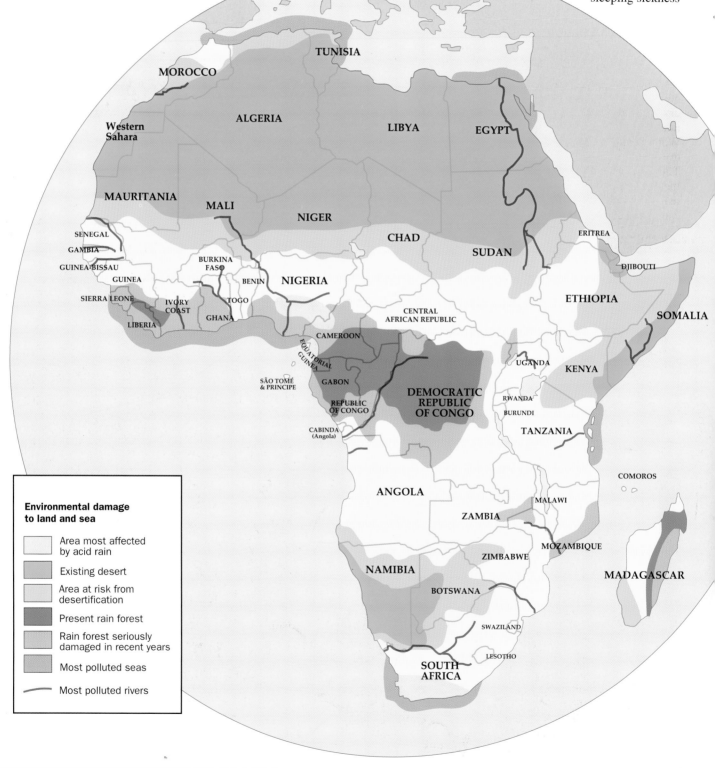

TUNISIA

MOROCCO

Western Sahara

ALGERIA

LIBYA

EGYPT

MAURITANIA

MALI

NIGER

CHAD

SUDAN

ERITREA

SENEGAL

GAMBIA

GUINEA-BISSAU

BURKINA FASO

DJIBOUTI

GUINEA

BENIN

NIGERIA

SIERRA LEONE

IVORY COAST

TOGO

GHANA

CENTRAL AFRICAN REPUBLIC

ETHIOPIA

SOMALIA

LIBERIA

CAMEROON

EQUATORIAL GUINEA

SÃO TOMÉ & PRINCIPE

GABON

UGANDA

KENYA

REPUBLIC OF CONGO

DEMOCRATIC REPUBLIC OF CONGO

RWANDA

BURUNDI

CABINDA (Angola)

TANZANIA

COMOROS

ANGOLA

MALAWI

ZAMBIA

MOZAMBIQUE

ZIMBABWE

MADAGASCAR

NAMIBIA

BOTSWANA

SWAZILAND

LESOTHO

SOUTH AFRICA

Environmental damage to land and sea

Area most affected by acid rain

Existing desert

Area at risk from desertification

Present rain forest

Rain forest seriously damaged in recent years

Most polluted seas

—— Most polluted rivers

Damaging the Environment

The destruction of the natural plant life in any area exposes the soil. When forests are cut down to create farmland, the rain dissolves plant nutrients in the soil. As a result, exposed soil in tropical rainy areas soon becomes infertile. Farmers then need to add expensive fertilizers to the soil to grow crops.

In dry areas, people graze cattle, sheep, and goats. The larger the herds, the greater the destruction of the plants on which the animals feed. The herders also need fuel, so they cut down trees and shrubs. As the numbers of people and animals in dry grassland areas increase, so the rate of plant destruction increases. When the plants are removed, the dry soil is broken up into fine dust. This dust is often blown away by the wind or washed away by storms, leaving bare rock on which nothing can grow. This is called soil erosion.

Natural Hazards

Unreliable rainfall and occasional long droughts are major natural hazards in Africa. Droughts lasting several years have occurred in the Sahel. Already scarce vegetation, unable to support an increasing population of people and livestock, has been stripped to bare earth and rock. This process, called desertification, turns once fertile land into desert. The people must migrate or starve. Other hazards include diseases, such as malaria, sleeping sickness, and AIDS. Diseases disable and kill millions of cattle and people.

Natural hazards and diseases

▢	Earthquake zones
▨	AIDS widespread
🦟	Malaria widespread
🪰	Sleeping sickness widespread
✴	Areas recently affected by famine

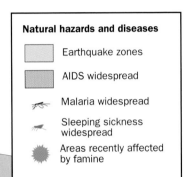

Endangered Species

Only 50 years ago, the forests and grasslands of Africa supported enormous numbers of wild animals. But the rapid increase in Africa's population has led to widespread destruction of forests and savanna regions once occupied only by animals. Many countries have set up national parks to conserve wildlife. These parks are tourist attractions, providing income as well.

Many animals have been killed for food or for profit. Poachers slaughter elephants for their ivory, and animals are killed when warfare damages their habitat. For example, in the eastern Democratic Republic of Congo, the endangered mountain gorillas were threatened by conflicts in the 1990s.

Black rhino

Some endangered species of Africa

Birds
Hermit ibis
Congo peacock
Mauritius kestrel
White-necked picathartes

Mammals
African hunting dog
Aye-aye
Black rhino
Grevy's zebra
Mountain gorilla

Marine mammals
Leatherback turtle

Plants
Afrormosia tree
Madagascar periwinkle
Mulanje cedar
Giant protea

ECONOMY

Africa has many natural resources, including oil and natural gas and huge deposits of valuable metals and precious stones. Most of the fuels and minerals are exported, however, because Africa lacks the industries to process them. About 60 percent of Africa's people live by farming. Many farmers are poor, producing little more than they need to support their families.

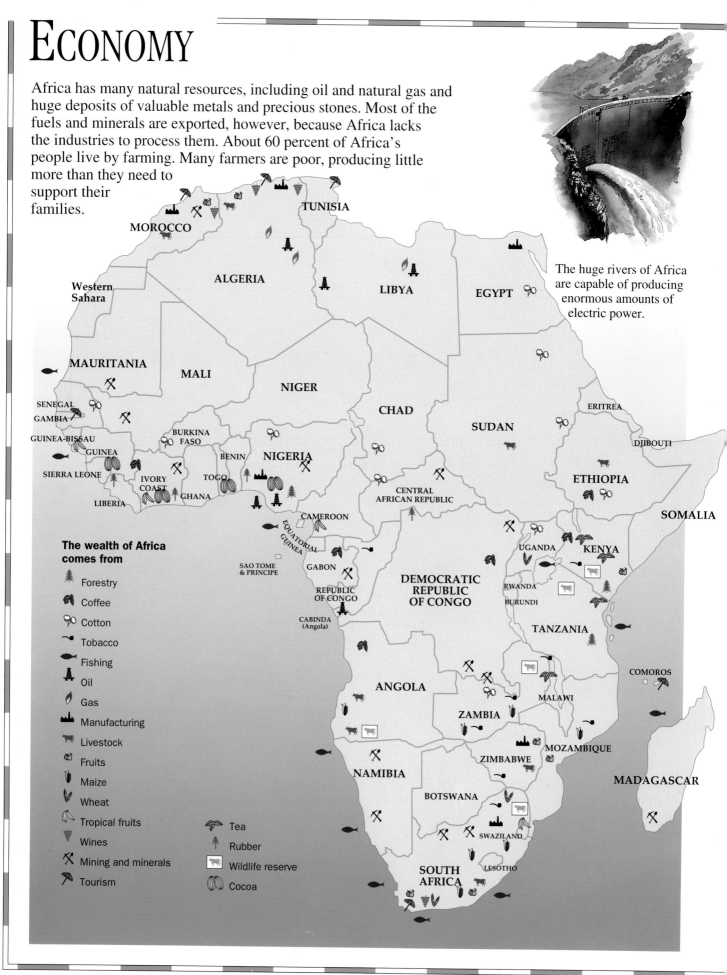

The huge rivers of Africa are capable of producing enormous amounts of electric power.

The wealth of Africa comes from

- Forestry
- Coffee
- Cotton
- Tobacco
- Fishing
- Oil
- Gas
- Manufacturing
- Livestock
- Fruits
- Maize
- Wheat
- Tropical fruits
- Wines
- Mining and minerals
- Tourism
- Tea
- Rubber
- Wildlife reserve
- Cocoa

MOROCCO
TUNISIA
ALGERIA
Western Sahara
LIBYA
EGYPT
MAURITANIA
MALI
NIGER
CHAD
SUDAN
ERITREA
SENEGAL
GAMBIA
GUINEA-BISSAU
BURKINA FASO
GUINEA
BENIN
NIGERIA
DJIBOUTI
SIERRA LEONE
IVORY COAST
TOGO
GHANA
CENTRAL AFRICAN REPUBLIC
ETHIOPIA
LIBERIA
CAMEROON
SOMALIA
EQUATORIAL GUINEA
SAO TOME & PRINCIPE
GABON
UGANDA
KENYA
REPUBLIC OF CONGO
DEMOCRATIC REPUBLIC OF CONGO
RWANDA
BURUNDI
CABINDA (Angola)
TANZANIA
COMOROS
ANGOLA
MALAWI
ZAMBIA
MOZAMBIQUE
ZIMBABWE
NAMIBIA
MADAGASCAR
BOTSWANA
SWAZILAND
SOUTH AFRICA
LESOTHO

Gross National Product

In order to compare the economies of countries, experts work out the gross national product (GNP) of the countries in U.S. dollars. The GNP is the total value of all the goods and services produced in a country in a year. The pie chart, right, shows that South Africa's GNP is the highest in Africa. It is a bit less than twice as large as Egypt's, the country with the second highest GNP. South Africa and Egypt are the most industrialized African countries.

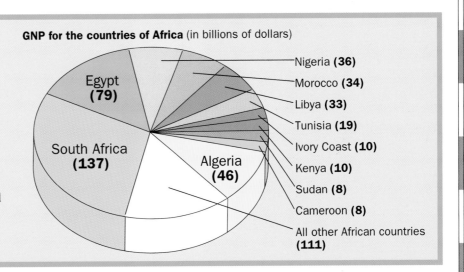

GNP for the countries of Africa (in billions of dollars)

Egypt (79)
South Africa (137)
Algeria (46)
Nigeria (36)
Morocco (34)
Libya (33)
Tunisia (19)
Ivory Coast (10)
Kenya (10)
Sudan (8)
Cameroon (8)
All other African countries (111)

Sources of energy

Although Africa lacks coal, several countries produce oil and natural gas. Major exporters include Nigeria, Libya, and Algeria. Egypt is another oil producer, but it uses most of its oil. Algeria, Africa's leading producer of natural gas, is one of the world's top ten producers. South Africa is Africa's only major producer of coal.

Hydroelectricity (water power) is important in countries with long rivers. For example, a major hydroelectric plant is located at the Aswan High Dam on the Nile River, Egypt. The Democratic Republic of Congo, Ghana, and Mozambique also have large hydroelectric power projects, while Zambia and Zimbabwe share the Kariba Gorge hydroelectric complex on the Zambezi River.

Per capita GNPs

Per capita means per head or per person. Per capita GNPs are worked out by dividing the GNP by the population. South Africa's per capita GNP is US $3,310, much lower than the United States' per capita GNP of $29,240. But many African countries are even poorer, with extremely low per capita GNPs. For example, the per capita GNP of Burund is only $140.

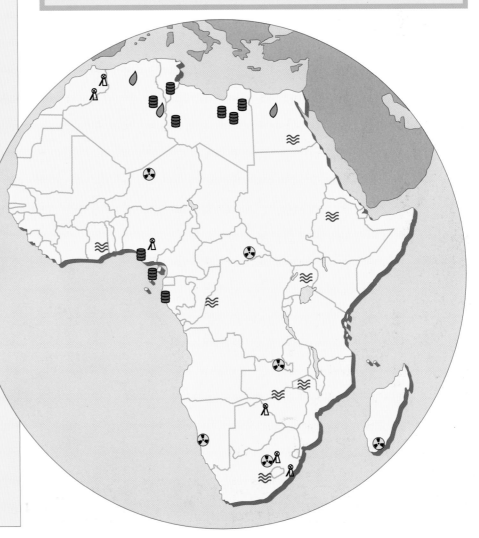

Sources of energy found in Africa

- Oil
- Gas
- Hydroelectricity
- Coal
- Uranium

POLITICS AND HISTORY

Africa contains 53 independent countries. Morocco in North Africa and Lesotho and Swaziland in southern Africa are monarchies. Morocco occupies Western Sahara, but some local people believe that it should be a separate, independent country. Most African countries are republics, though many are not fully democratic.

Since achieving independence, the progress of many countries has been slowed by instability. Civil wars and military takeovers have occurred in many countries, with military leaders replacing civilian governments.

Great Events

Fossil evidence suggests that the evolution of the human species began in Africa.

Around 3100 BC, northeastern Africa was the site of a great early civilization, Ancient Egypt. In the Middle Ages, several major kingdoms, such as Ancient Ghana and Mali, flourished in West Africa. These kingdoms traded with the Arabs, who lived to the north and the east.

European influence south of the Sahara began in the 15th century. At first, Europeans seldom went inland. Instead, they traded for slaves, gold, and other valuable goods on the coast. In the late 19th century, most of Africa came under European rule. But starting in the 1950s, the countries of Africa gradually won their independence. In 1994, South Africa held its first multi-racial elections Nelson Mandela was elected president.

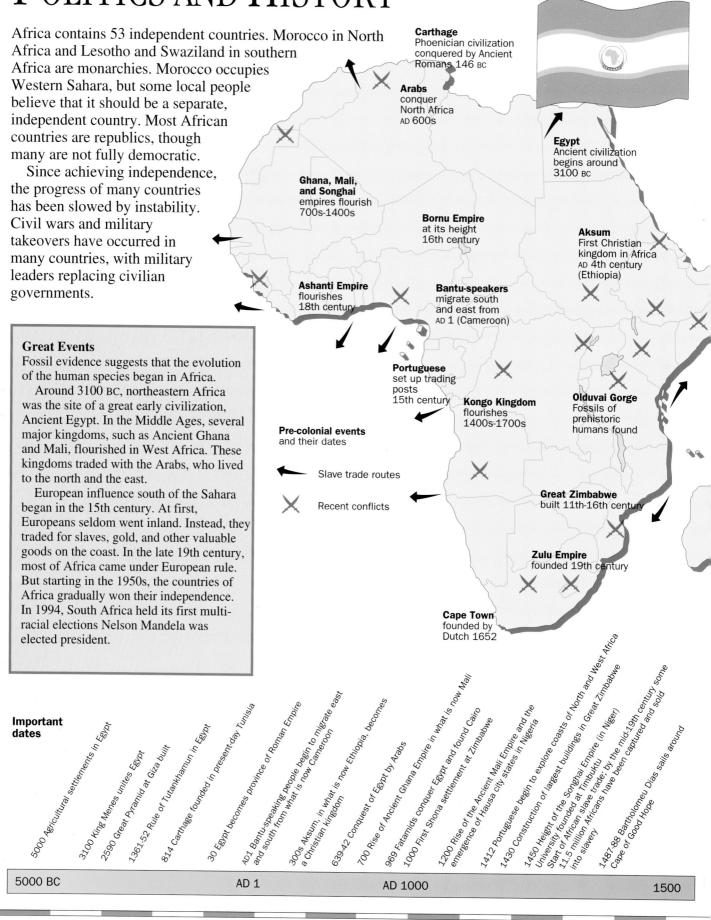

Carthage
Phoenician civilization conquered by Ancient Romans 146 BC

Arabs
conquer North Africa AD 600s

Egypt
Ancient civilization begins around 3100 BC

Ghana, Mali, and Songhai
empires flourish 700s-1400s

Bornu Empire
at its height 16th century

Aksum
First Christian kingdom in Africa AD 4th century (Ethiopia)

Ashanti Empire
flourishes 18th century

Bantu-speakers
migrate south and east from AD 1 (Cameroon)

Portuguese
set up trading posts 15th century

Kongo Kingdom
flourishes 1400s-1700s

Olduvai Gorge
Fossils of prehistoric humans found

Pre-colonial events
and their dates

→ Slave trade routes

✕ Recent conflicts

Great Zimbabwe
built 11th-16th century

Zulu Empire
founded 19th century

Cape Town
founded by Dutch 1652

Important dates

5000 Agricultural settlements in Egypt

3100 King Menes unites Egypt

2590 Great Pyramid at Giza built

1361-52 Rule of Tutankhamun in Egypt

814 Carthage founded in present-day Tunisia

30 Egypt becomes province of Roman Empire

AD1 Bantu-speaking people begin to migrate east and south from what is now Cameroon

300s Aksum, in what is now Ethiopia, becomes a Christian kingdom

639-42 Conquest of Egypt by Arabs

700 Rise of Ancient Ghana Empire in what is now Mali

969 Fatamids conquer Egypt and found Cairo

1000 First Shona settlement at Zimbabwe

1200 Rise of the Ancient Mali Empire and the emergence of Hausa city states in Nigeria

1412 Portuguese begin to explore coasts of North and West Africa

1430 Construction of largest buildings in Great Zimbabwe

1450 Height of the Songhai Empire (in Niger) University founded at Timbuktu

Start of African slave trade; by the mid-19th century some 11.5 million Africans have been captured and sold into slavery

1487-88 Bartholomeu Dias sails around Cape of Good Hope

| 5000 BC | AD 1 | AD 1000 | 1500 |

44

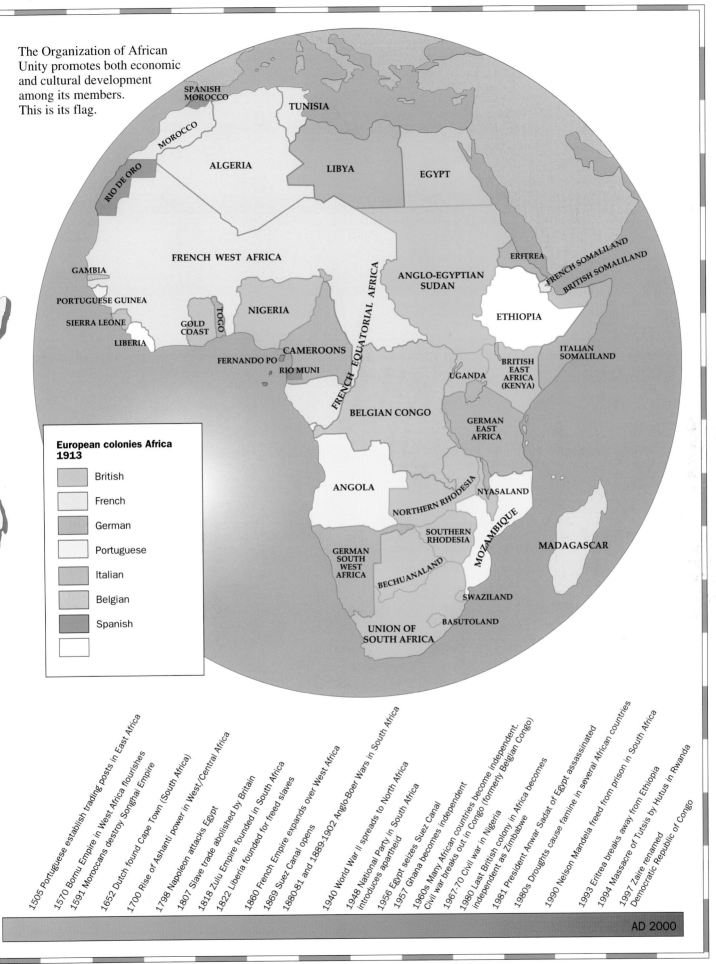

The Organization of African Unity promotes both economic and cultural development among its members. This is its flag.

European colonies Africa 1913

- British
- French
- German
- Portuguese
- Italian
- Belgian
- Spanish

SPANISH MOROCCO
TUNISIA
MOROCCO
RIO DE ORO
ALGERIA
LIBYA
EGYPT
FRENCH WEST AFRICA
ERITREA
FRENCH SOMALILAND
BRITISH SOMALILAND
ANGLO-EGYPTIAN SUDAN
GAMBIA
PORTUGUESE GUINEA
SIERRA LEONE
LIBERIA
NIGERIA
TOGO
GOLD COAST
ETHIOPIA
ITALIAN SOMALILAND
CAMEROONS
FERNANDO PO
RIO MUNI
FRENCH EQUATORIAL AFRICA
UGANDA
BRITISH EAST AFRICA (KENYA)
BELGIAN CONGO
GERMAN EAST AFRICA
ANGOLA
NORTHERN RHODESIA
NYASALAND
MOZAMBIQUE
SOUTHERN RHODESIA
MADAGASCAR
GERMAN SOUTH WEST AFRICA
BECHUANALAND
SWAZILAND
BASUTOLAND
UNION OF SOUTH AFRICA

1505 Portuguese establish trading posts in East Africa
1570 Bornu Empire in West Africa flourishes
1591 Moroccans destroy Songhai Empire
1652 Dutch found Cape Town (South Africa)
1700 Rise of Ashanti power in West/Central Africa
1798 Napoleon attacks Egypt
1807 Slave trade abolished by Britain
1818 Zulu Empire founded in South Africa
1822 Liberia founded for freed slaves
1860 French Empire expands over West Africa
1869 Suez Canal opens
1880-81 and 1889-1902 Anglo-Boer Wars in South Africa
1940 World War II spreads to North Africa
1948 National Party in South Africa introduces apartheid
1956 Egypt seizes Suez Canal
1957 Ghana becomes independent
1960s Many African countries become independent
1967-70 Civil war breaks out in Congo (formerly Belgian Congo)
1980 Last British colony in Africa becomes independent as Zimbabwe
1981 President Anwar Sadat of Egypt assassinated
1980s Droughts cause famine in several African countries
1990 Nelson Mandela freed from prison in South Africa
1993 Eritrea breaks away from Ethiopia
1994 Massacre of Tutsis by Hutus in Rwanda
1997 Zaire renamed Democratic Republic of Congo

AD 2000

INDEX

Numbers in **bold** are map references
Numbers in *italics* are picture references

Picture credits
Photographs; AS Publishing *9*
The Hutchinson Library 6, 11, 12, 15, 18, 20, 25, 29, 30, 33
Travel Photo International 27, 34